THE RELIGIONS OF CHINA.

CONFUCIANISM AND TÂOISM DESCRIBED

AND

COMPARED WITH CHRISTIANITY.

BY

JAMES LEGGE,

PROFESSOR OF THE CHINESE LANGUAGE AND LITERATURE IN THE
UNIVERSITY OF OXFORD.

HODDER AND STOUGHTON,
27, PATERNOSTER ROW.
—
MDCCCLXXX.

THE SPRING LECTURE

OF THE

PRESBYTERIAN CHURCH OF ENGLAND

FOR 1880.

DELIVERED IN THE COLLEGE, GUILFORD STREET, LONDON.

WHEN asked by the Rev. Dr. Dykes, on behalf
of the Committee of the Presbyterian College,
to write and deliver the following Lectures,
the author was the more ready to accede to
his request because he does not himself belong
to the Presbyterian Church. He longs to see
a frequent interchange of services among
ministers of different churches, who are in
cordial sympathy in the faith and love of their
common Lord.

CONTENTS.

LECTURE I.

CONFUCIANISM.

Meaning in these lectures of the name Confucianism—
Error of not regarding Confucius as a religious
teacher—The earliest thoughts on religion of the
Chinese to be sought in their primitive written
characters—Primitive for heaven or the sky—For
the name God—For spirits and spiritual things—
For the idea of manifestation or revelation—For the
spirits or manes of departed men—Three primitives
relating to divination—Results derived from the
primitive characters and further method of treating
the subject—The old religion of China was not
merely animistic, with a fetishist tendency—Views
of Professor Tiele—What took place in the time
between the formation of the primitive characters
and the twenty-third century B.C.—Institution of a
worship of God and a worship of ancestors—The
Shû King, and its evidence concerning the worship
of Yâo and Shun as a monotheism, with an inferior
worship of spirits—Testimony of the Shih King,
in addition to the Shû—Predicates in them both
about Heaven and Shang Tî, or God—New style of
speech on the rise of the Châu dynasty, in the twelfth

LECTURE II.

CONFUCIANISM.

The worship of their forefathers by all the Chinese people —Filial piety—The worship of parents a part of it— Filial piety and worship of Shun ; and subsequently down to the Châu dynasty—Living representatives of the dead then employed—Further description of the filial piety and worship of the Châu kings—Titles

Contents.

LECTURE III.

TÂOISM.

LECTURE IV.

THE RELIGIONS OF CHINA COMPARED WITH CHRISTIANITY.

I.

CONFUCIANISM: ITS DOCTRINE AND WORSHIP OF GOD.

郊社之禮所以事上帝也

"In the ceremonies at the altars of Heaven and Earth, they served God."—*Confucius, "Doctrine of the Mean,"* ch. xix.

"They knew God."—*Paul, Romans* i. 21.

I.

The meaning in these Lectures of the name Confucianism.

1. THE first thing to be done in these Lectures is to give an account of Confucianism, and I must define at the outset in what sense I wish that term to be understood. No name current among men is more fully historical than that of Confucius. We know the years, and the months, and the days of the months, in which he was born and died. We see him moving on the stage of his country for between seventy and eighty years in the sixth and fifth centuries before our Christian era. But the religion of China does not date only from his time. It has been said, indeed, but incautiously, that "without Confucius, China had been without a native religion."[1] The sage, no doubt, helped to preserve the ancient religion of his country, and it may be said that it took some tinge through him from his own character and views; but more than

[1] " Studies in the Philosophy of Religion and History." A. M. Fairbairn. Page 244.

this cannot be affirmed. What he claimed for himself was to be a "transmitter, and not a maker, believing in and loving the ancients;" that "he was fond of antiquity, and earnest in seeking knowledge there."[1] What his grandson claimed for him was that "he handed down (the doctrines of) Yâo and Shun, as if they had been his ancestors, and elegantly displayed (the regulations of) Wăn and Wû, taking them as his models."[2]

I use the term Confucianism, therefore, as covering, first of all, the ancient religion of China, and then the views of the great philosopher himself, in illustration or modification of it, —his views as committed to writing by himself, or transmitted in the narratives of his disciples.[3] The case is pretty much as when we comprehend under Christianity the records and teachings of the Old Testament as well as those of the New.

The error of not regarding Confucius as a religious teacher.

Thus much in vindication of my extended application of the name Confucianism, and in

[1] "Confucian Analects," VII., i., xix.
[2] "Doctrine of the Mean," xxxi.
[3] See my Preface to Vol. III. of the "Sacred Books of the East," pp. xiv., xv.

correction of the error of some who think of Confucius in connexion with the religion of China more highly than we have reason to think. A few words on an error in regard to him of an opposite character will not be out of place. The questions have often been put to me, " But is Confucianism really a religion ? Was it anything more than a system of morals intended for the government of human society ? " The most extended expression of this sentiment is given in a recent number of *The China Review,* where the writer says, " Confucianism pure and simple is in our opinion no religion at all. The essence of Confucianism is an antiquarian adherence to traditional forms of etiquette,—taking the place of ethics ; a sceptic denial of any relation between man and a living God,—taking the place of religion ; while there is encouraged a sort of worship of human genius, combined with a set of despotic political theories. But who can honestly call this a religion ? "[1] Certainly if this were a fair account of all there is in Confucianism, I would not call it a religion.

[1] *The China Review,* Vol. VIII., i., p. 59. See also the previous number, p. 363, where the Rev. Mr. Macintyre says, " Confucius was a sceptic, who deemed it his duty to conceal his scepticism out of deference to the ancient sages and traditional opinions." See also Note A.

But the representation is absurdly unfair. I will not stop to show this immediately. I think you will all agree with me in what I thus say of it, when I come to show what the teachings of the Chinese sage, " pure and simple," were.

The earliest thoughts of the Chinese on religion to be sought for in their primitive written characters.

2. I will now give a view of some of the religious thoughts of the fathers of the Chinese people, the fruit of which is found in the beliefs of their descendants down to the present day. In doing this, I will go back to a period long anterior to the composition of the most ancient Chinese books, and glance with you at some of the primitive written characters. We shall get from them a vivid idea of what was in the minds of those fathers when they were laying the foundations on which so great a structure of literature has been built by their descendants. We shall be in the position of the Aryan philologists, who, from the root-words of Sanskrit and other kindred languages, try to give us pictures of the earliest Aryan life ; as, for instance, when Professor Max Müller, in his " Essay on Comparative Mythology," having found the root of daughter (duhitar) in duh, meaning to milk,

goes on to observe, " The name of milkmaid, given to the daughter of the house, opens before our eyes a little idyll of the poetical and pastoral life of the early Aryans." [1]   We are not treading on less firm ground when we undertake to do the same for the ancient Chinese by the study of their primitive characters. We are, in fact, treading on much firmer ground. Hunting for roots in the fields of philology is difficult and uncertain. What a boon it would be if a chart were discovered somehow of the root-words of that speech which existed somewhere before it branched out into Sanskrit, Celtic, Latin, Greek, Teutonic, and the other languages that claim to be descended from it ! Such a chart we have of what we may call Chinese roots in its primitive characters,—the pictures and ideagrams which exhibit to the student by the eye the ideas in the minds of their makers. We thus learn their meaning without reference to the names by which they have been called,[2] and, according to the sentiment of the line in which Tennyson condenses two well-known lines of Horace :

" Things seen are weightier than things heard."

[1] " Chips from a German Workshop," II., p. 26.

[2] See two papers on " Principles of Composition in Chinese as deduced from the Written Characters," in the *Journal of the Royal Asiatic Society*, Vol. XI., Part ii. New Series.

Application of the above method.

3. Let me therefore adduce a few specimens of those primitive characters which served as the symbols of the religious or supersensuous notions of their makers, and which are still employed to classify, or assist in the pronunciation of, hundreds of other characters of later formation. It is by unbroken tradition from the earliest historic time that we determine their meaning; —if we could exactly make out their pictorial outlines and original grouping, we should see how that meaning grew from their component parts. The results of analysis, so far as they go, are remarkable, and put us *en rapport* with the Chinese fathers fully five thousand years ago.[1] From no other source do we obtain information so important and reliable concerning what we may call the religion of infant man.

Primitive for heaven or the sky.

i. Our first example shall be the character t'ien, the symbol for h e a v e n. Its application must have been first to the visible sky, but, all along the course of history, it has also been used as we use H e a v e n, when we intend the ruling Power, whose providence embraces all.

[1] See Note B.

The character is made up of two other primitives—yî, the symbol of unity, placed over tâ, the symbol of great,[1] and thus awakens the idea of the sky, which is above and over all, and to whose magnitude we can assign no limit.[2]

Professor Max Müller says: "In Chinese, t'ien denotes sky or day, and the same word, like the Aryan dyu, is recognized as the name of God."[3] But it was the vastness of the sky, and not its brightness, which made the *sensus numinis* in the ancient Chinese use its name to express the idea of an overruling Power. There was a radical difference in the concepts of the Aryan and Chinese fathers, supposing that our view of those concepts is correct. That of the former might be symbolized by Apollo ; that of the latter, by Hercules. And, moreover, the Chinese did not from t'ien, " the sky," fashion a character or name which should be used as the general appellation God, and lead the mind to the Supreme Being as a person.

Primitive for the name God.

ii. That name was Tî, and the character so denominated is the second primitive of which

[1] 天 (t'ien) = 一 (yî = one) over 大 (tâ = great).

[2] See Note C.

[3] " Lectures on the Science of Language," II., p. 480.

I wish to speak. It is more complex in form than t'ien, and native help fails us in the attempt to analyse it into its constituent parts and ascertain their significance.[1] There is no doubt, however, as to the idea which it was made to symbolise,—that, namely, of " lordship and government."[2] Heaven is styled Shang Tî,. and as frequently Tî alone without the Shang.   That addition, meaning Supreme, individualises and exalts the Tî ; and throughout the Shû and the Shih, the ancient books of History and Poetry, the names T'ien, Tî, and Shang Tî are constantly interchanged,—in the course of the same chapter or paragraph, often in the same sentence.   Tî enters also into the title of the emperor of China, Hwang Tî meaning " the great or august Tî."   This shows how adapted it is for an appellative name ; but such application of it is only two thousand years old, and dates from B.C. 221, when it was adopted by the founder of the shortlived dynasty of Ch'in, avowedly that he might appear equal to Fû-hsî, and other ancient sovereigns, to whom the title of Tî had been given in subsequent times by a process of deification.   Since its earliest formation, Tî has properly been the personal name of Heaven.   T'ien has had much of the

[1] See Note D.   [2] See Note E.

force of the name Jahve, as explained by God Himself to Moses; Tî has presented that absolute deity in the relation to men of their lord and governor. Tî was to the Chinese fathers, I believe, exactly what God was to our fathers, whenever they took the great name on their lips.

Thus the two characters show us the religion of the ancient Chinese as a monotheism. How it was with them more than five thousand years ago, we have no means of knowing; but to find this among them at that remote and early period was worth some toilsome digging among the roots or primitive written characters. I will only add here that the relation of the two names which we have been considering has kept the monotheistic element prominent in the religion proper of China down to the present time, and prevented the prostitution of the name Tî, as Deus and other corresponding appellations of the Divine Being were prostituted.

Primitive ch'î, used for spirits, and spiritual things.

iii. I proceed to a third primitive symbol, having two different names or pronunciations, ch'î and shih.[1] Pronounced ch'î, it is used as

---

[1] 示, composed of 二 and 小.

the significant element in characters denoting spiritual beings, sacrifices, and prayer. Spirits generally, and especially those whose seat is referred to heaven, are called shăn;[1] those whose influence is in and over the earth are simply styled ch'i, and an altar to them is called sheh,[2] formed from ch'i and t'û, signifying "the ground," "territory;" and another character altogether, of which I will presently speak, is employed for the spirits or *manes* of departed men.

Primitive shih, with the idea of manifestation or revelation.

Pronounced shih, this character is the symbol for manifestation and revelation. The upper part of it is the same as that in the older form of Tî, indicating "what is above;" but of the three lines below I have not found a satisfactory account. Hsü Shăn says they represent "the sun, moon, and stars," and that the whole symbolises "the indications by these bodies of the will of Heaven." Shih therefore tells us that the Chinese fathers believed that there was com-

---

[1] 神, composed of 示 and the phonetic 申

[2] 社, composed of 示 and 土.

munication between Heaven and men. The idea of revelation did not shock them. The special interpretation of the strokes below, however, if it were established, would lead us to think that even then, so far back, there was the commencement of astrological superstition, and also, perhaps, of Sabian worship.

Primitive for the spirits, or manes, of departed men.

iv. I have just said that another character is used for the spirits, or *manes*, of departed men. It is named k w e i,[1] and enters into the characters corresponding to the Latin *anima* and *animus*, or the animal soul and the intelligent ; besides being an extensively used phonetic element. According to Hsü Shăn, it is formed from the figure of a ghost's or demon's head over the legs of a man, with the addition of another character, denoting maliciousness. Tâi scouts this analysis of it, and deservedly so ; but he supplies no better himself. I cannot form a definite idea of what the makers meant by using this k w e i as the symbol of the disembodied spirit. We learn from it, however, that they did not think

---

[1] 鬼, formed of 甶 (a ghost's head), 儿 (the legs), and 厶 (selfish).

that man when he was dead, had all ceased
to be.

Three primitives relating to divination.

v. There are still three other primitives,
affording us some insight into the religious
notions of the earliest Chinese, on which I will
make a few observations. They are connected
together, the two last being derived from the
first.

That first character is named p û,[1] and is the
symbol for divining by the lines produced through
a certain process on the back of a tortoise-shell.
It consists merely of two lines, which may pos-
sibly have been intended to represent the lines
appearing on the shell. For some reason or other
the makers held the tortoise-shell in veneration,
and supposed that it possessed a mysterious
power of indicating, with regard to undertakings
about which it was consulted, whether their issue
would be fortunate or unfortunate.

The second character is kwâ,[2] with p û as its
significant element, and used itself as a phonetic.
It was the symbol for divining by means of the
eight famous trigrams of Fû-hsî, themselves

---

[1] 卜, or 卜.

[2] 卦, formed from 圭 and 卜.

called " the eight Kwâ." They are not characters, but lineal figures on which was built up
the mysterious book called the Yî King. Its
diagrams were worked in divination by manipulating a certain number of stalks from a plant
called the shih, the *Ptarmica Sibirica.*[1] The
formation of kwâ from pû, and the absence of any
primitive character for this plant, indicate that this
method of divination was more recent than that
by the tortoise-shell, though we find them both
recognized in the " Counsels of the Great Yü,"
one of the oldest documents of the Shû King.

The third character, also formed from pû, by
the addition of (k'âu,)[2] the symbol for a mouth, is
chan, which is one of the most fruitful phonetic
elements, and gives its name to more than
seventy characters. It was the symbol for the
interpretation of the answers given by the shell
divination, the practice of which, it would appear,
was reduced to some sort of art. The interpretation of the answers derived from the stalks
was expressed by a character shî, not so ancient
as chan, and composed of the symbol for the
bamboo, and another denoting a sorceress or

[1] So, Dr. Williams. See his Syllabic Dictionary, on
the character Shih (蓍).

[2] 占, formed from ⼘ , (pû), and 口 (k'âu).

spirit-medium. Superstition had found its way
very early into the minds of the ancient Chinese,
and made itself manifest side by side with the
intelligence that appeared in the characters for
Heaven and God.

I may have seemed tedious while dwelling so
long on the testimony borne to the ancient
religion of China by its primitive written characters; but the conclusions which I have drawn
from it are legitimate and important. I felt
their truth soon after I began the study of the
language here in London, nearly forty-three
years ago; but many years elapsed before I saw
my way to set them forth as I have endeavoured
to do to-day.

**Results derived from the primitive charac-
ters, and further method of treating the
subject.**

4. Five thousand years ago the Chinese were
monotheists,—not henotheists, but monotheists;
and this monotheism was in danger of being
corrupted, we have seen, by a nature worship on
the one hand, and by a system of superstitious
divination on the other. It will be my object to
show, first, how the primitive monotheism has
been affected by these dangers in the course of
time, and how far it has prevailed over them.

I will then speak of the worship of ancestors, and of the departed great, as it has prevailed in the country. My third subject will be the place of man considered as to his nature, duty, and destiny in the religion of China ; and, finally, I will give you, if the time permit me, and according to my lights, a sketch of the life and character of Confucius and of his teachings, so far as they have not appeared in our discussion of the other subjects. One Lecture will not suffice for all this, but I hope to accomplish it in two.

The old religion of China was not merely animistic with a fetishist tendency.— Views of Professor Tiele.

5. I may appropriately introduce the first of these four subjects by referring to a view of the old religion of China that has recently found expression in Europe, and places it in the category of what are called animistic religions. Professor Tiele of Leiden says : " The religion of the old Chinese empire, as it existed certainly from the twelfth century B.C., and probably at a much earlier period, is best described as a purified and organised worship of spirits, with a predominant fetishist tendency, combined into a system before it was possible for a regular mythology to develop out of it. The sole

2

objects of worship are the spirits (shăn), which
are divided into heavenly, earthly, and human,
and, as a rule, are still closely connected with
the objects of nature." [1]

What religion, it may be asked, is not
animistic, in the sense that its objects of worship
are regarded as spirits? But it is not merely
because they are spirits that they are worshipped, but because of the relation that they
are supposed to sustain to the worshippers, and
to the Supreme Spirit, or God. If the old
Chinese religion were only animism, whence
came it to have, as far back as we can go, Tî or
God as the one supreme object of its homage?
And as to the other spirits, to whom at an early
period an inferior worship was paid, and who,
it is said, were closely connected with the
objects of nature, they were worshipped as
doing service to men on behalf of God. In
default of prayers or hymns of a date anterior
to our era addressed to such spirits, we may
accept, as representing faithfully the ancient
tradition, the following prayers to the heavenly
and earthly spirits, selected from the " Statutes
of the Ming dynasty (1368—1642)." To the

[1] " Outlines of the History of Religion to the Spread of
the Universal Religion," p. 27. (Trübner and Co., 1877.
Translated by J. Estlin Carpenter, M.A.)

heavenly spirits, "the spirits of the Cloud-master, the Rain-master. the lord of the Winds, and the Thunder-master," it is said, "It is your office, O Spirits. to superintend the clouds and the rain, and to raise and send abroad the winds, as ministers assisting Shang Tî. All the people enjoy the benefits of your service."[1] Again, to the earthly spirits, "the spirits of the mountains and hills, of the four seas and four great rivers, of the imperial domain, and of all the hills and rivers under the sky," it is said, "It is yours, O Spirits, with your Heaven-con-ferred powers, and nurturing influences, each to preside as guardian over one district, as ministers assisting the great Worker and Transformer, and thus the people enjoy your meritorious services." Such language might seem to have been con-structed to prevent the misrepresentation that the religion of China took its form from the principle of animism.

Professor Tiele says that in the ancient Chinese worship of spirits there was a pre-dominant fetishist tendency. Perhaps he means by this no more than what he says in the next sentence, that the spirits were still closely connected with the objects of nature. But

[1] See my "Notions of the Chinese concerning God and Spirits," pp. 34, 35. (Hong-kong, 1852.)

according to the prayers just read, they were so connected with those objects in subordination to the conception of nature as sustained by Shang Tî, or God, for the good of mankind, having its different parts, with their elemental agencies, committed to the guardian care of the spirits. This is not our view of nature, but it is one that has appeared in different stages of society; and I do not see any tendency to fetishism in it. There is a danger, indeed, of the spiritual potencies being regarded as independent, and being elevated to the place of gods ; but the most ancient and strong conviction of one God prevented this in China.

But the language of Professor Tiele may have been moulded by a mental reference to the wooden tablets which are employed as resting-places for the spirits, both in the state worship of China and the ancestral. These are small rectangular pieces of wood, at least as high again as they are wide, set up in front of the worshipper, and having written upon them the characters shǎn wei, "Seat of the spirit," or ling wei, "Seat of the soul," or shǎn chù, "Lodging-place of the spirit," with, perhaps, the surname, name, and office of the departed, in the ancestral worship. While the worship is performed, the tablet is supposed to be occupied by the spirit specially interested in the service; and at the conclusion, the spirit returns to its own place, and the tablet is laid aside in its repository, till required for use again, being in the interval no more spirit-possessed than any other piece of wood.[1] In the next Lecture I shall have to speak of the practice, especially during the Châu period, of using living members of the worshipping family, to be taken possession of by the spirits of the deceased, instead of these wooden tablets. How the use of the tablet originated, can only be matter of speculation with us, and I will not take up time with an attempt to account for it. But it was not and is not fetishism. "A fetish," says Professor Max Müller, "properly so called, is itself regarded as something supernatural; the idol was originally meant as an image only, a similitude or a symbol of something else. No doubt, an idol was apt to become a fetish; but, in the beginning, fetish-worship, in the proper sense of the word, springs from a source totally different from that which produces idolatry."[2]

[1] See Note F.
[2] Lectures (the Hibbert) on the Origin and Growth of Religion, as illustrated by the Religions of India, pp. 63, 64.

The tablet is not regarded as in itself either supernatural or sacred ; and it has operated to prevent the rise of idolatry in the Confucian religion of China,—a fact to which I may have occasion to refer hereafter.

What took place in the time between the formation of the primitive characters and the twenty-third century B.C.— Institution of a worship of God, and a worship of Ancestors.

6. From what we may call the prehistoric time, in which we have found great exercises of thought, we arrive at the twenty-third century before our era. More than a thousand years have passed since Fû-hsî, during which period there must have been growth and development, both progress and corruption. We know very little of what was transacted in that millennium on the theatre of China. A few hints are given by later historians ;—we do not know on what authority. A few are given also by Confucius himself, in the longest of the appendixes to the Yî King, ascribed to him ; but however willing we may be to accept them as his, both they, and a few other similar passages in "the Record of Rites," crumble away, on close handling, into speculations and guesses about the progress of

society. One very important step had certainly been taken during the long and unreported interval. Methods of worship, as the complement of the religious ideas on which I have tried to throw light from the primitive Chinese characters, had been instituted: a worship of God for all, but in which the ruler of the State should be the only officiator; and a worship of ancestors by all, or at least by the Heads of families, for themselves and all the members in their relative circle. The nature of this twofold worship will fully appear as I proceed. At the present day we find the state worship of God, and the universal worship of ancestors, and we can trace them back from dynasty to dynasty. If we cannot fully explain every modification which they underwent, we are certain that we always have substantially the same things before us, until we reach the time immediately succeeding the prehistoric.

The Shû King, and its evidence concerning the worship of Yâo and Shun as a monotheism, with an inferior worship of spirits.

7. We come to the Shû King, a compilation of historical documents, and the oldest of Chinese books. The first two parts of it extend over a

hundred and fifty years, and are occupied with
the characters and events of the sage rulers—Yâo
and Shun.[1]   I do not say that the composition
of them was contemporaneous with, or immediately subsequent to, the things that they
narrate ; but there is an element of history in
them.   They bear the *imprimatur* of Confucius,
and will repay our careful examination.   A very
intelligent Chinese gentleman, now in Europe,
said to me, not very long ago, " We have nothing
in China the roots of which are not to be found
in the Canons of Yâo and Shun."

In the Canon of Shun we have the record of
several acts of religious worship.   Yâo resigns
the administration of the government to Shun,
and his inauguration in that new position takes
place "in (the temple of) the Accomplished
Ancestor."[2]   That ancestor, I suppose, was he
to whom Yâo traced his lineage, and his sanction
was thus sought for the transference of the
kingdom to another.   Shun was now the ruler
of the Chinese state, and he signalised the fact
by a solemn act of worship: " He sacrificed
specially, but with the ordinary forms, to Shang

[1] Yâo's reign began in B.C. 2357, and Shun's ended in
2207.   The shorter chronology of the Bamboo books
reduces these dates, but only by a little more than two
hundred years.

[2] The Shû, II. i. 4.

Tî,"—that is, we have seen, to God; "sacrificed purely to the six objects of Honour; offered their appropriate sacrifices to the hills and rivers, and extended his worship to the host of spirits."[1]

The notice that Shun, on this occasion, when sacrificing specially to God, yet used the ordinary forms, indicates that there was even then a regular worship of God by the sovereign of China,—such, no doubt, as we find fully established in later times, and observed at the present day. Thereafter, every fifth year, on his tours of inspection through his dominions, Shun offered what seems to have been a similar sacrifice at each of the four quarters of the country, where he met the feudal lords, "presenting," as it is expressed, "a burnt-offering to Heaven, and sacrificing in order to the hills and rivers."[2] When he returned from these tours to the capital, "he went to (the temple of) the Cultivated Ancestor, and offered a single bullock."[3]

It is impossible to give a distinct account of the other sacrifices offered by Shun, when he undertook the administration of the government. Chinese writers differ among themselves in what

---

[1] The Shû, II. i. 6.   [2] *Ib.*, i. 8.
[3] *Ib.*, i. 8.

they say about "the six objects of Honour."
When he sacrificed to the hills and rivers, he
did so to the spirits supposed to preside over
the hills and rivers of note in all the kingdom,
and thereby exercised his royal prerogative, for
in subsequent ages each feudal lord sacrificed to
the hills and rivers in his state, while the worship of the sovereign embraced all such objects
"under the sky."[2] The final statement that
Shun "extended his worship to the host of
spirits," is understood of all spirits not attended
to in his previous sacrifices,—"those," it is said,
"presiding over mounds, dykes, plains, and
forests, and the spirits of the sages and worthies
of ancient times."[3]

Thus in the worship of the sage Shun, we see
the primitive monotheism of his race, and that
there had grown up round it an inferior worship of multitudinous spirits. I have already
argued that this inferior worship was not a
nature-worship, and that it was subordinate to
the homage due to God, and resulted from
a mistaken idea of His government in creation.
This will be seen more fully as we go on.

[1] See note in the Chinese Classics, Vol. II., *in loc.*, and
" Mayers' Chinese Reader's Manual," p. 329.
[2] The Lî Chî, xx. 3.
[3] See Commentary in the Yung-chăng Shû, *in loc.*

Testimony of the Shih King in addition to the Shû.—Predicates in them both about Heaven and Shang Tî, or God.

8. The documents of the Shû extend, though not continuously, over between seventeen and eighteen centuries. Next in antiquity to the Shû is the Shih, or book of ancient poetry. It contains three hundred and five pieces, six of which are of the period of the second feudal dynasty, from B.C. 1766 to 1123. The rest are of the third or Châu dynasty, down into the sixth century B.C.

In both of these books many things are predicated of Heaven, Tî, and Shang Tî, that are true only of the true God. He is the ruler of men and all this lower world. Men in general, the mass of the people, are His peculiar care. He appointed grain to be the chief nourishment of all. He watches especially over the conduct of kings, whom he has exalted to their high position for the good of the people. While they reverence Him, and fulfil their duties in His fear, and with reference to His will, taking His ways as their pattern, He maintains them, smells the sweet savour of their offerings, and blesses them and their people with abundance and general prosperity. When they become impious and negligent of their duties, He punishes them, takes away the throne from them, and appoints others in their place. His appointments come from His fore-knowledge and fore-ordination.

Sometimes He appears to array Himself in terrors, and the course of His providence is altered. The evil in the state is ascribed to Him. Heaven is called unpitying. But this is His strange work, in judgment, and to call men to repentance. He hates no one; and it is not He who really causes the evil time : that is a consequence of forsaking the old and right ways of government. In giving birth to the multitudes of the people, He gives them a good nature, but few are able to keep it, and hold out good to the end.

There is a remarkable document of the Shû, called "The Establishment of Government," in which the consolidator and legislator of the Châu dynasty gives a summary of the history of the feudal kingdom down to his own time. Yü the Great, the founder of the Hsiâ dynasty, dating from B.C. 2205, "sought for able men who should honour God (in the discharge of their duties)." But the way of Chieh, the last of his line, was different. Those whom he employed were cruel men, and he had no successor. The kingdom

was given to T'ang the Successful, the founder
of the Shang or Yin dynasty, who "grandly
administered the bright ordinances of God."
His reign dates from B.C. 1766; but Shâu, the
last of his line, came to the throne in 1254, and
was cruel as Chieh had been. God, in consequence, "sovereignly punished him." The throne
was transferred to the House of Châu, whose
chiefs showed their fitness for the charge by
"employing men to serve God with reverence,
and appointed them as presidents and chiefs of
the people," while all their other ministers,
such as their officers of law, their treasurers
and historiographers, were "men of constant
virtue."[1]

Such is the testimony of the Shû and Shih
as to the views entertained concerning God
during the many centuries to which the histories
and pieces belong; nor do they contain a sentence inconsistent with those which I have woven
into my description; nor is there a word in them
about the sacrifices to other spirits implying
that there was one among them "equal or second"
to, or more than a minister of, Shang Tî.

[1] This and the two previous paragraphs are taken almost
verbatim from my prolegomena to the Chinese Classics,
II., pp. 193, 194, and III., p. 152. The original texts are
there indicated.

New style of speech on the rise of the
Châu dynasty, in twelfth century B.C.
—The dualistic phrase Heaven and Earth
used for the single Heaven, and Tî.

9. On the rise of the Châu dynasty we meet
with a style of speech that is new. Its first sovereign (B.C. 1122) in a "Great Declaration" made
to his adherents when he had taken the field
against the last ruler of Yin, said, " Heaven
and Earth is the parent (lit., the father and
mother) of all creatures, and of all creatures
man is the most intelligent. The sincerely
intelligent (among men) becomes the great
sovereign, and the great sovereign is the parent
(lit., the father and mother) of the people. But
now, Shâu, the king of Shang, does not reverence Heaven above, and inflicts calamities on
the people below." Heaven and Earth pass
immediately, you perceive, into the one name
Heaven ;—notwithstanding the dualistic form of
the expression, it is only one that is the parent of
all creatures.[1] Further on in the "Declaration,"
we have similar and still more remarkable language, corrected in the same way by reference

---

[1] The Shû, V. i., sect. r., 3, 4, " Heaven and Earth " is
no more plural, than the sovereign, who also is " father
and mother," is plural.

to the one supreme controlling Power, to whom the speaker gives the name of Heaven. The phrase "Heaven and Earth" stands for the Being sacrificed to at the two places distinguished as the altars to heaven and earth;—at the round altar to heaven on the day of the winter solstice, and at the square altar to earth on the day of the summer solstice. Such was the practice under the Châu dynasty as it is at the present day. There was a danger of its leading to serious misconception concerning the oldest religious ideas and worship of the nation, —a danger which Confucius himself happily came in to avert. We have from him the express statement that "the ceremonies of the sacrifices to Heaven and Earth are those by which we serve Shang Tî."[1] The worship offered in them was to the one and the same God.

Expansion of the judgment of Confucius about the two sacrifices by the author.

A commentator expands this sentence of the sage in the words,[2] "The emperor sacrifices to

---

[1] "The Doctrine of the Mean," xix. 6.
[2] See the Four Books, with the Standard Commentary and a Paraphrase, *in loc.*

heaven on the round mound at the winter
solstice, and at the summer solstice to the
earth at the square pool. Thus service is
performed to Shang Tî, and the emperor
takes the sincerity and reverence wherewith
he gives honour to heaven and respect to the
earth to acknowledge His goodness in the
processes of production and maturing." The
meaning which we are thus led to attach to
the two ceremonies is the following, and I
state it now in words which I used eight-and-
twenty years ago : "The material heavens and
earth are the great works of God. They speak
to man with different voices, and utter con-
cordant, yet various, testimony concerning their
maker. When we consider the heavens, we
are filled with awe ; we are moved to honour
and reverence Him whose throne they are.
When we consider the earth, we are pene-
trated with a sense of His kindness. Softer
feelings enter into the soul, and we are disposed
to love Him who crowneth the year with His
goodness. The heavens are to us the representatives of the Divine majesty; the earth is
the representative of the Divine care. The
former teaches us God's more than paternal
authority ; the latter His more than maternal
love. By means of the one and the other we

rise to Him, as maintaining a sovereign rule and an ever-watchful care; as the Being into our service of whom there should enter the elements of fear and love, reverence and gratitude. Such is the ideal of the highest worship in the religion of China, the worship rendered through the services at the summer and winter solstices."[1]

Some may suppose that I have expressed myself about it as from a Christian standpoint; they will hardly do so when they hear some prayers to Shang Tî, in which Chinese devotion reached its height.

How the dualistic name continued, and is guarded against being misunderstood. —Announcement by the first emperor of the present dynasty.

10. We will come to them soon; meanwhile let me say that the judgment of Confucius must be accepted as final on the common object of the two solstitial services. Unfortunately, his words did not have the effect of abolishing the use of the double name,—Heaven and Earth, instead of Heaven or God; yet the abuse is for the most part rendered harmless by the more correct phraseology with which it is associated.

[1] "Notions of the Chinese concerning God and Spirits," p. 51.

Let me give an example. In 1644, when the
first emperor of the present dynasty took possession formally of the throne, he announced
the fact at a great service to Heaven in a prayer
which began thus :—

" I, the Son of Heaven, of the Great Pure
dynasty, humbly, as a subject, dare to make
announcement to imperial Heaven and sovereign
Earth. Throughout the vast world, God looks
on all without partiality. My imperial grandfather received the gracious decree of Heaven,
and founded a kingdom in the east, which
became firmly established. My imperial father,
succeeding to the kingdom, established it, and
it grew wider and more powerful. I, Heaven's
servant, in my poor person, became the inheritor
of the dominion they transmitted." Further on,
he says : " I, receiving Heaven's favour, and in
agreement with the wishes of the people, on
this the first day of the tenth month, announce
to Heaven that I have ascended the throne of
the empire." Evidently in this announcement,
" imperial Heaven and sovereign Earth," was but
a periphrasis for the names God and Heaven,—
Heaven, whose servant the Emperor was.[1]

[1] See the whole prayer in Edkins' " Religion in China,"
pp. 18, 19.

The Yî King, and its subject-matter.

11. I should be glad now to adduce at once the prayers of which I spoke a little ago; but it is necessary to say something about the Yî King, "the mysterious book." In 1876 a translation of it was published by the Rev. Canon M'Clatchie, M.A., of Shanghâi, with Notes and Appendix. Another translation in Latin, with still more copious notes, made in the first part of last century by Father Regis and other Jesuit missionaries, had been published at Stuttgart in 1834, edited by the late Jules Mohl. The difference between the two versions is considerable; the difference of opinion between the two translators as to the bearing of the book on the question of the Religion of China is very great indeed. The writer of an article in the *Edinburgh Review* for October, 1877, based on Canon M'Clatchie's translation, says that the Yî King is "the fountain-head to which we must go to gain a true notion of the deeper beliefs" of the Chinese; and adds that if Ricci, the pioneer of Roman Catholic missionaries in China, and certainly one of the ablest of them, —"if Ricci had read the works of Chû-tsze. and the Yî King, he never would have imagined that the T'ien, the Heaven of the Confucianist's

worship, had any points of similarity with the
Christian's God." I have no doubt that Ricci
had " read, marked, and inwardly digested " the
Yî, and only found his conclusions respecting
the religion of China, drawn from other sources,
confirmed by it. So it has been with myself.
The reviewer quotes a sentence from Mr.
M‘Clatchie to the effect that " so long as comparative mythology continues to be neglected
by Chinese students, so long must the Yî King
remain a sealed book to them." I cannot admit
that, as Chinese students, I, and others who
think with me, have neglected comparative
mythology. I have looked much into it, but I
have looked more into the Yî itself. It would
be passing strange if Confucius, with all his
appendixes to it, had not been able to make
its meaning sufficiently plain without our re-
sorting to writings much more recent than
itself, and whose authors had never heard of
it. What, then, do we find in the Yî ? Before
I answer this question, let me point out an
error into which the Canon and his reviewer
equally fall. The latter calls the Yî "the
oldest book of the oldest nation; " and the
former, "the most ancient of the Chinese
classical writings." [1] The fact is, that not a

single character in the Yî is older than the twelfth century B.C. The text of it, not taking in the appendixes of Confucius, consists of two portions,—from king Wăn, and from his son, the duke of Châu. The composition of Wăn's portion is referred to the year 1143 B.C. As an authority for the ancient religion of China, therefore, the Yî is by no means equal to the Shû and the Shih.

In these circumstances, how has the common opinion about the antiquity of the book arisen? The answer is, that it is based on diagrams, or lineal figures, ascribed to Fû-hsî, and made up of whole and divided lines (——— and — —). Those figures are in all sixty-four, but the prevailing opinion is that only eight of them were from

Fû-hsî,—the famous kuâ or trigrams (———,

———, ———, ———, — —, — —,

— — — —). What their framer intended by these figures we do not know. No doubt there was a tradition about it, and I am willing to believe that it found a home in the existing Yî. There is some ground also to suppose that there was an explanation, or two explanations, of the figures during the two dynasties that

preceded Châu. If there were, the whole has
perished. If king Wăn and his son incorpo-
rated previous explanations with their own, so
important a fact could hardly have escaped
special mention.

The character called Yî is the symbol for the
idea of change. The Yî is "The Book of
Changes." The fashion of the world is continually being altered. We have action and
reaction, flux and reflux,—now, one condition,
and immediately its opposite. The vicissitudes
in the worlds of sense and society have their
correspondencies in the changes that take place
in the lines of the diagrams. Again, certain
relations and conditions of men and things lead
to good, are fortunate ; and certain others lead
to evil, are unfortunate ; and these results are
indicated by the relative position of the lines.
Those lines were systematically changed by
manipulating with a fixed number of the stalks
of a certain plant. In this way the Yî served
the purpose of divination; and since such is
the nature of the book, a reader must be prepared for much in it that is tantalizing, fantastic,
and perplexing.

The whole lines in the figures are styled the
strong, and the divided lines the weak. The
two represent the two forms of the subtle matter

—whether eternal or created is not said—of which all things are composed. Under one form the matter is active, and is called yang; under the other it is passive, and is called yin. Whatever is strong and active is of the yang nature; whatever is weak and passive is of the yin. Heaven and earth, sun and moon, light and darkness, male and female, ruler and minister, are examples of these antinomies. The aggregate of them makes up the totality of being; and the Yî is supposed to give, in its diagrams, a complete picture of the phenomena of that totality. It does not give us a sexual system of nature, though of course the antinomy of sex is in it; but the lines on which it is constructed embrace other antinomies as well. Authority and power on the one side; inferiority and docility on the other:—these are the ruling ideas in the Yî. Mr. M'Clatchie makes the sexual antinomy unpleasantly prominent, both in his translation and his notes.[1]

Further, the hidden operation in and through which the change takes place in nature is said to be that of the kwei shăn. We have seen that kwei was the name for the spirit of departed men,[2] and shăn[3] the name for spirits

---

[1] See Note H. [2] Page 13.
[3] Page 12.

generally, and specially for spirits of heaven. The combination of the names can often be translated in no other way than by spirits, spiritual beings. In the Yî, however, its signification is held to be peculiar and technical. Shăn is yang, and indicates the primary matter in the process of expanding; kwei is yin, and indicates the same in the process of contracting. But we shall see, immediately, that Confucius held there was a force in the operation which was not material.

What I have thus said about the Yî has given you, I hope, an inkling of the nature of the work, and I cannot devote more time to it. It is a book of strange physical speculation, constructed so as to serve the purpose of divination, and affords us little help in studying the subject of religion.

On the divination of the old Chinese.

12. Let me interject here a few sentences on the divination of the Chinese. I showed how a superstition on the subject had infected the minds of the earliest fathers, and that this was proved by some of the primitive characters. It should be understood, however, that it was not supposed that by means of divination future events in themselves could be known before-

hand. Its object was to determine what would be the issues of undertakings contemplated by the consulter, and how certain anticipated conditions of events would turn out;—whether they would be fortunate or unfortunate, lucky or unlucky. And we are told that the tortoise-shell and the stalks were consulted only in doubtful cases. But the whole scheme was vain, and must have been injurious to the practical conduct of life. The old methods of divination have fallen into disuse, and I cannot say how far other methods are sanctioned by the Government; but the almanac published with its approval still contains the distinction of days as lucky for this enterprise and that, and unlucky for that enterprise and this. With the multitudes, divination is still a popular profession. Those who follow it are for the most part Tâoists, if they are anything in religion.

Appendixes by Confucius to the Yî.—Two sentences from one of them.

13. The larger portion of the text of the Yî is understood to be from Confucius himself. His opinion of it was very high, and he said that if his life were prolonged, he would give fifty years to the study of the Yî. In what he wrote about it two objects at least clearly appear:—

to impart a moral and ethical character to its
lessons ; and to explain how the lineal figures
were made to represent the phenomena of
change in nature.   In his appendix called
" Discourses on the Diagrams," he describes
the processes of Tî, as emblemed by the eight
trigrams, throughout the four seasons, until,
as the Lord and Master, He has crowned the
year with His goodness.   The whole passage
has always brought to my mind Thomson's
Hymn to the Seasons.

I will end my account of the Yî by quoting
two sentences from the longest of the appendixes.   The one of them expresses the substance of the book in these few words : " The
successive movement of the inactive and active
elements makes what is called the course (of
things in nature)."   The other sentence is
equally brief: " That which is unfathomable
in (the movement of) the inactive and active
elements is what we call (the presence of a)
spiritual (operation)."   Confucius felt that all
which appeared in the Yî did not account for
all that took place in the world of fact.   Given
the distinction of the states of matter into
inactive and active; given also the agencies
of expansion and contraction ;—there was, after
all, something unfathomable in every pheno-

menon, and in that unfathomableness the sage recognized the working of a spiritual power. When my mind first apprehended his meaning, there came into it also those words of the apostle Paul, " The same God worketh all in all." In a wider application than the apostle had in view, Confucius felt, I believe, that in all phenomena there was the presence and doing of God, the potency that "spreads undivided and operates unspent," an immanent spirit, and yet not to be confounded with the matter which He moulds and changes.[1]

Prayers to Shang Tî at a special solstitial sacrifice in A.D. 1538.

14. I am now free to draw to a close this branch of my subject on the monotheism of the Chinese as seen in the state worship, by submitting to you a series of prayers addressed to Shang Tî, in the year 1538, by the then emperor of the Ming dynasty. They suit my purpose, perhaps, better than any other selection of solstitial prayers that could be made, because they were prepared for a special occasion. It had been determined to make a slight change in the name by which the Supreme Being was called in the imperial worship. Heretofore the

See Note I.

name had been, "Shang Tî, (dwelling in the) bright heavens;" henceforth it should be "Shang Tî, (dwelling in the) sovereign heavens."[2] Such was the matter canvassed at Peking, while in London, at the court of Henry VIII., they were deliberating about the articles of the new creed to be given to the nation instead of the dogmas of the Church of Rome. The change was made. It was inaugurated at a solemn service with more than the formalities of a regular grand sacrifice; and the style then initiated passed over without alteration into the worship of the present Tartar dynasty.

But such a thing could not be done without various preparation,—in heaven as well as on earth. The intercession with Shang Tî of all the spirits in any way associated with the solstitial worship must be secured, and for this purpose the emperor went in state to the round altar, and heard the reading of the following paper :—

"I, the emperor of the Great Illustrious dynasty, have respectfully prepared this paper to inform—the spirit of the sun; the spirit of the moon; the spirits of the five planets, of the constellations of the zodiac, and of all the stars in all the sky; the spirits of the clouds, the

[2] See Note K.

rain, wind, and thunder ; the spirits which have
duties assigned to them throughout the whole
heavens ; the spirits of the five grand mountains ; the spirits of the five guardian hills ;
the spirits of the five hills, Chî-yün, Hsiang-
shăng, Shăn-lieh, T'ien-shân, and Shun-teh ;
the spirits of the four seas ; the spirits of the
four great rivers : the intelligences which have
duties assigned to them on the earth ; all the
celestial spirits under heaven ; the terrestrial
spirits under heaven ; the spirit presiding over
the present year ; the spirit ruling over the
tenth month, and those over every day ; and
the spirit in charge of the ground about the
border altar.

"On the first day of the coming month, We
shall reverently lead our officers and people to
honour the great name of Shang Tî, dwelling
in the sovereign heavens, looking up to the
lofty nine-storied azure vault. Beforehand we
inform you, all ye celestial and all ye terrestrial
spirits, and will trouble you, on our behalf, to
exert your spiritual power, and display your
vigorous efficacy, communicating our poor desire
to Shang Tî, and praying Him graciously to
grant us His acceptance and regard, and to be
pleased with the title which we shall reverently
present.

"For this purpose we have made this paper for your information. All ye spirits should be well aware of our purpose. Ye are respectfully informed."

This paper shows how there had grown up around the primitive monotheism of China the recognition and worship of a multitude of celestial and terrestrial spirits ; and yet the monotheism remained. Shang Tî stands out, not among, but above all, those spirits, single, alone. They are but ministering spirits, and though there are occasions when worship is paid to them specially, they receive their orders from the emperor, who speaks to them, as he does to his ministers and people, with the authoritative We.

But I hasten on. The selected day arrived, and we stand, with the emperor and his suite, at the round altar. We watch and listen to them while they engage in the different parts of their service,—as eleven times they prostrate themselves in reverent homage. First, they greet the approach (real, they think, though invisible) of the spirit of Shang Tî, and say: "Of old, in the beginning, there was the great chaos, without form and dark. The five elements had not begun to revolve, nor the sun and moon to shine. In the midst thereof there presented itself neither form nor sound. Thou, O spiritual Sovereign, camest forth in Thy presidency, and first didst divide the grosser parts from the purer. Thou madest heaven; Thou madest earth; Thou madest man. All things got their being, with their reproducing power." [1]

The next step was to present a notice about the change in the title, when it was said: " O Tî, when Thou hadst opened the course for the inactive and active forces of matter to operate, Thy making work went on. Thou didst produce, O Spirit, the sun and moon, and five planets; and pure and beautiful was their light. The vault of heaven was spread out like a curtain, and the square earth supported all on it, and all creatures were happy. I, Thy servant, presume reverently to thank Thee, and, while I worship, present the notice to Thee, O Tî, calling Thee Sovereign."

Precious stones and silks were then presented as offerings, with the following prayer: " Thou hast vouchsafed, O Tî, to hear us, for Thou regardest us as our Father. I, Thy child, dull and unenlightened, am unable to show forth my

---

[1] See for all the prayers here my " Notions of the Chinese," pp. 25 to 31. I think "madest" is the likeliest word in English for the character lî in this prayer. It is the symbol of setting up, establishing.

feelings. I thank Thee that Thou hast accepted the intimation. Honourable is Thy great name. With reverence we spread out these precious stones and silk, and, as swallows rejoicing in the spring, praise Thine abundant love."

Vessels with offerings of food followed, with this prayer: "The great feast has been set forth, and the sound of our joy is like thunder. The Sovereign Spirit vouchsafes to enjoy our offering, and his servant's heart is within him like a particle of dust. The meat has been boiled in the large caldrons, and the fragrant provisions have been prepared. Enjoy the offering, O Tî, and then shall all the people have happiness. I, Thy servant, receiving Thy favours, am blessed indeed."

A first drink-offering was now made, when it was said: "The great and lofty One sends down His favour and regard, which we, in our insignificance, are hardly sufficient to receive. I, His simple servant, while I worship, present this precious cup to Him, whose years have no end."

There was next a thanksgiving in these words: "When Tî, the Lord, had so decreed, He called into existence[1] the three powers

---

[1] The character whose meaning I have thus expressed is very strong. Translators of our Scriptures into Chinese

(heaven, earth, and man). Between heaven and earth He separately disposed men and things, all overspread by the heavens. I, His small servant, beg His (favouring) decree, to enlighten me His vassal; so may I for ever appear before Him in the empyrean."

At a second drink-offering it was said: "All the numerous tribes of animated beings are indebted to Thy favour for their beginning. Men and creatures are emparadised, O Tî, in Thy love. All living things are indebted to Thy goodness, but who knows whence his blessings come to him? It is Thou alone, O Lord, who art the true parent of all things."

There was a third and final drink-offering, when it was said: "The precious feast is wide displayed; the gem-adorned benches are arranged; the pearly spirits are presented,—with music and dancing.[1] The spirit of harmony is collected; men and creatures are happy. The breast of His servant is troubled, that he can make no recompense (for such goodness)."

After this, the various offerings were removed, and it was said: "The service of song is com-

have uséd it, alone or with another character, for the Hebrew *bara*.

[1] These have always been accompaniments of the great religious services.

4

pleted, but our poor sincerity cannot be fully
expressed.   Thy sovereign goodness is infinite.
As a potter hast Thou made all living things.
Great and small are curtained round (by Thee
from harm).   As engraven on the heart of Thy
poor servant is the sense of Thy goodness, but
my feeling cannot be fully displayed.   With
great kindness Thou dost bear with us, and,
notwithstanding our demerits, dost grant us life
and prosperity."

It remained only to send away the spirit of
Shang Tî, and to burn the various offerings.   At
the performance of these ceremonies, the following prayers were used: "With reverent ceremonies the record has been presented; and Thou,
O Sovereign Spirit, hast deigned to accept our
service.   The dances have all been performed,
and nine times the music has resounded.   Grant,
O Tî, Thy great blessing to increase the
happiness of my House.   The instruments of
metal and precious stones have given out their
melody ; the jewelled girdles of the officers have
emitted their tinklings.   Spirits and men rejoice
together, praising Tî the Lord.   What limit,
what measure can there be, while we celebrate
His great name ?   For ever He setteth fast the
high heavens, and establisheth the solid earth.
His government is everlasting.   His poor

servant, I bow my head, and lay it in the dust, bathed in His grace and glory."

And finally: "We have worshipped and written the Great Name on this gem-like sheet. Now we display it before Tî, and place it in the fire. These valuable offerings of silks and fine meats we burn also, with these sincere prayers, that they may ascend in volumes of flames up to the distant azure. All the ends of the earth look up to Him. All human beings, all things on the earth, rejoice together in the Great Name."

Conclusions from those prayers.

15. I will not multiply words to try and increase the impression which these prayers must have made upon your minds. The original monotheism of the Chinese remains in the state worship of to-day. We saw how the fathers of the nation, when they began to form their written characters, figured the visible heavens as the one thing over and above all, and illimitable. Then there arose in their minds the idea of God, ruling and overruling all, symbolized to them by the figure of this visible sky. Their name for this idea of God conceived of as a personal being was Tî, and the connexion between the two names T'ien and Tî, Heaven

and God, tended to prevent the rise of polytheism, and to bring about the extrusion of it,
if it did at any time manage to obtain a foothold
in the religion of the country. Whether it ever
did do so, and if it did, in what manner the
thing came about, are questions on which neither
the time nor my inclination will permit me to
enter. All semblances of an uncertain polytheism
were swept away from the imperial worship
soon after the middle of our fourteenth century,
immediately on the rise of the Ming dynasty,
whose statutes have supplied us with a series of
such remarkable prayers. We may not be able
to feel much sympathy with the way in which
the solstitial services are conducted. We may
deplore, as we do deplore, the superstitious
worship of a multitude of spirits, terrestrial and
celestial, that finds a place in them ; but this
abuse does not obscure the monotheism. Those
spirits are not Gods, and are not called by the
divine name. As I have already said, I do not
think that, in the truly Confucian worship of
the empire, that name, the name Tî, is applied
to any spirit but Him whose right it is. As
well might we argue that Roman Catholicism
is not monotheistic, because of the place which
is held in it by angels and saints, as that the
religion of China is not so because of the inferior

worship given in it to various spirits, real or fictitious.

16. With some remarks on the nature of the offerings at the solstitial services, and the absence of a priestly class from the Chinese religion, I will bring this Lecture to a close.

The offerings at the solstitial services are oblations, not propitiatory sacrifices.

These offerings are oblations, and not sacrifices in our common acceptation of that term. There is not, and never was, any idea of propitiation or expiation in them. They are the tributes of duty and gratitude, accompanied with petitions and thanksgivings. They do not express a sense of guilt, but the feeling of dependence. A whole burnt-offering, indeed, consumed on a special furnace near the altar, always forms a part of the greatest solstitial services; but the sins of the emperor and people have not been confessed over the head of the heifer so devoted. It does not bear those sins in its body, nor in its death carry them away. The idea of substitution is not in the solstitial or in any other of the religious services of the Chinese people; nor is the idea of consecration on the part of the worshipper symbolized by any part of the worship.

**The idea of substitution is not unknown
in Chinese history, but has no place
in the religious services.**

17. We have in the Shû a document of the date
B.C. 1766.   In it T'ang, a truly noble and heroic,
and I venture to say also, pious man, having
overthrown the dynasty of Shang, announces to
his subjects the principles of the rule through
which they would, under himself, enter on a new
life.   At the conclusion of it, he said, "When
guilt is found anywhere in you who occupy the
myriad regions, let it rest on me, the One man.
When guilt is found in me, the One man, it shall
not attach to you who occupy the myriad
regions."   In harmony with this generous utterance was an incident in the life of T'ang, which,
though not in the Shû, has been handed down
by the historian Sze-mâ Ch'ien and others.
For seven years after his accession (B.C. 1766
—1760), there was a great drought and famine.
It was suggested at last by some one that a
human victim should be offered in sacrifice to
Heaven, and prayer made for rain.   T'ang said,
" If a man must be the victim, I will be he."
He fasted, cut off his hair and nails, and in a
plain carriage, drawn by white horses, clad in
rushes, in the guise of a sacrificial victim, he

proceeded to a forest of mulberry trees, and there prayed, asking to what error or crime of his life the calamity was owing. He had not done speaking when a copious rain fell. The ideas of substitution and consecration are thus to be found in the history of China, but they have not found their way into its religious ceremonies.

The solstitial service is an acknowledgment by the emperor for himself, and his line, and the nation, of their obligations to God.

18. Writing with reference to the solstitial services, Dr. Edkins says that "the idea of a sacrifice in them is that of a banquet."[1] This is hardly intelligible. The notion of the whole service might be that of a banquet; but a sacrifice and a banquet are incompatible ideas. Nor is the idea of a banquet altogether appropriate to a solstitial service. It is true that the ancestors of the emperor are present, that is, are supposed to be present, in spirit, on the altar, and receive homage from him, thus being assessors of Shang Tî, and sharing with him in the tribute of the service; but they are there only from the deep

[1] "Religion in China," p. 23.

conviction of the solidarity of the family, which is characteristic of the Chinese. They and their descendants are the representatives of the family which was called by the divine decree to rule the empire when the sovereigns of the previous dynasty had been proved incompetent to fulfil that high charge. The highest title of the living chief of the family is that he is "the son of Heaven," the one man whom Heaven delights to honour, as if he were Its first-born son, and to whom is delegated the duty of ruling the myriads of the people for their good, in harmony with the divine will.

The emperor stands forth in his dignity, and his glory is reflected on his ancestors, present with him in spirit, and who have been the steps, each in his own time and place, by which the dignity came to him. But the whole service is to Shang Tî, and the last act of it is the burning of the offerings and prayers, that their smoke may ascend in a cloud of incense to heaven. The emperor, for himself and his line, and as representing all the millions of his subjects, gives in it solemn expression of their obligations to God, and of their purpose to rule so as to secure the objects intended by Him in the institution of government. Such is my idea of the highest acts of worship in the religion of China.

The emperor does not preside at the services as a priest.

19. It is often said that at the solstitial services the emperor appears at once the high priest and the father of the people. But if he be the high priest, who are the class of priests under him? There is no priesthood in China. We apply improperly to the religious offerings in its various services the name of sacrifices, and then conclude that in order to offer those sacrifices there must be priests.[1]

Ancient division of the Chinese community into four classes, with no indication of a priesthood.—The place of that supplied, to some extent, by the cultured class.

The distinction of all the Chinese community into four classes is very ancient. It is named in one of the books of the Shû[2] as an existing division in the twelfth century B.C. The four classes were the official or cultured class, the husbandmen, the mechanics or workers, and the traders or merchants. This was a social, and not a religious, distribution of the community; and owing to it there never appeared in China

---

[1] See note L.   [2] V. xx. 12.

anything like the castes of Brahmanism. The official or cultured class have, all along the line of Chinese history, borne some resemblance to a clerical body. While the feudal system lasted, the members of this class were scions of the princely families of the different states, who had been educated in the schools set apart for them, and the shadowy forms of which we can dimly discern nearly four thousand years ago. When the element of rank disappeared from the community, that of education was developed and took its place. The literati generally became the ruling class, or the class from which, as a rule, the governors of the people should be chosen. They come nearest to our idea of a clerical body; but they are far enough from being priests, or even in any sense ministers of religion, unless when they are exercising some function in connexion with the state worship. The emperor himself presides at the highest services of that worship as a minister of religion, giving expression to the highest ideas of God that have been the inheritance of his nation for several millenniums, and acknowledging the dependence of all upon Him for life and breath and all things; but he does this as the parent and representative of the people, and not as a priest.

NOTES TO LECTURE I.

NOTE A, p. 5.

In the Buddhist work, "A Dispassionate Discussion of Confucianism (lit., the system of the Learned), Buddhism and Tâoism," by the recluse ascetic, Liû Mî, it is said that "the great idea in Confucianism is correctness," and that its object is "the right ordering of society." This would reduce it to a system of morals and manners. The author did not understand what religion is. Confucianism is the only one of the three systems he treats of, from which he could have got an idea of this. His discussion, of course, comes to a triumphant issue in favour of Buddhism ; but the book might in many respects be a model for controversialists.

NOTE B, p. 8.

I am speaking within bounds when I say that by these characters we go back five thousand years. Their invention is ascribed to Fû-hsî, Ts'ang Chieh, and Hwang Tî. The first year of Hwang Tî was B.C. 2697 ; but, according to the chronologists, the evidence preponderates in favour of Fû-hsî (see the largest of the appendices to the Yî King, ascribed to Confucius, Pt. ii. 23, and the preface to the Shû King, by his descendant K'ung An-kwo), as the inventor of the written characters. The "Chronological Tables from the Twenty-four Histories," published with authority early in the present century, make Fû-hsî's reign begin in B.C. 3252. They give another estimate making the year B.C. 3697, and a third which would place it at a still more distant date.

The " Chronological tables of the reigns throughout the different dynasties," published in 1817 by Ch'î Shâonan, give B.C. 3376 for Fû-hsî's first year, placing also fifteen reigns between him and the Yen Tî, Shăn-năng shih, without saying how long they lasted.

From the tables in the Yî Sze, or " Lengthened Histories," by Mâ Sû of the present dynasty, the lowest estimate makes Fû-hsî's reign begin in B.C. 3316 ; but one estimate is mentioned which would carry him up to more than B.C. 20000 !

There is nothing extravagant, therefore, in placing the commencement of the written characters of China five thousand years back from the present time.   Dr. Morrison (View of China for Philological Purposes, p. 58) makes Fû-hsî's reign commence in B.C. 3369.   The late Mr. Mayers (Chinese Reader's Manual, p. 366) reduces the date to 2852 ; and he is followed by Dr. Edkins (Introduction to the Study of Chinese Characters, p. 2).   I have not been able to find any Chinese authority for this reduction.   The assigning to Shăn-năng only forty years is evidently an oversight.

NOTE C. p. 9.

Hsü Shăn, author of the Shwo Wăn dictionary, A.D. 100, says that t'ien was formed from yî and tâ, on the principle of " association of ideas."   Tâi T'ung, a lexicographer of our thirteenth century, takes the upper line as equivalent to " what is above," and refers the formation of t'ien to the principle of " indication."   His account of its significance, however, is substantially the same as that of Hsü Shăn, which I have followed in the Lecture. T'ien is also a phonetic element, though overlooked by

Callery, Williams, and Edkins. Dr. Williams even says (Syllabic Dictionary, Introduction, p. lxi.) on the ninety-first phonetic, " This primitive resembles t'i e n, heaven ; but that forms no derivatives." No derivatives ! In Chalmers' Concise Dictionary of Chinese, p. 268, t'i e n appears as a phonetic ; and, along with two other subordinate phonetics derived from it, it gives rise to forty different characters. It has all the characteristics of a primitive.

NOTE D, p. 10.

T î is written 帝, which is modified from a more ancient form. Hsü Shǎn and Tâi T'ung make the upper portion of it to indicate "what is above," but they give us no help towards analysing the rest. Dr. Chalmers (The Origin of the Chinese, p. 12) makes the whole equivalent to " He who is great, overruling heaven and earth." Whatever may be thought of this analysis, he introduces it with the important observation that " the peculiar nature of Chinese written language has done good service in stereotyping, so to speak, the primitive belief in one Supreme Tî." The " Concise Dictionary " shows forty-two other characters, in which Tî is the sole or partial phonetic element.

NOTE E, p. 10.

This is Tâi's account of Tî,—"the honourable designation of lordship and government." The recognition of the Supreme Being as our Lord and Governor is, I must believe, the true *sensus numinis* in the mind of man. It is not an intuition innate in his nature ; but it is a conviction that does not fail, in connexion with his perceptions, to arise in the unsophisticated mind. My firm persuasion of this has made me hold for many years

that the Chinese Tî and our God are synonymous terms
of the two languages ; and it keeps me from accepting,
without question, the meaning of the Sanskrit Deva,
identified with deus and other corresponding terms, in
the root significance of being "the bright or shining."
"The bright" may well be an epithet of God, as in the
old Chinese poem, "The bright and glorious Shang-Tî
(Shih, IV., Dec. ii., Ode 2,)" but could hardly be that
general appellation itself.

In illustration of this important point, I venture to give
two sentences from Sir Isaac Newton's famous scholium
at the end of his Principia : "Deus est vox relativa, et
ad servos refertur ; et deitas est dominatio Dei, non in
corpus proprium uti sentiunt quibus deus est anima mundi,
sed in servos. Deus summus est ens eternum, infinitum ;
sed ens, utcunque perfectum, sine dominio non est
dominus meus." There is a very remarkable reference
to this scholium at the commencement of Voltaire's
tractate on "The Metaphysics of Sir Isaac Newton.
(London, 1747. Translated by David Erskine Baker.)"

NOTE F, p. 21.

The most common name for this tablet is Shăn chû
(神 主). On this name Dr. Williams (Syllabic
Dictionary, p. 88) says,—"Shăn chû, the ancestral
tablet, intimating that the deified lord resides in it."
"Deified lord" is an erroneous translation of the characters for shăn and chû in the name. Shăn, according
to its proper significance, is here the symbol for the idea
of spirit, spirits, spiritual, and is used substantively,
="the Spirit." Chû is here not ="lord," though that is
a common meaning of the character. It is used as a
verb, in a well-known sense,—the symbol of residing with,
being present, as a guest (Mencius, V. i., ch. 8.). The

spirit is present at the service, a guest for the occasion. On every occasion of worship, the first prayer is "to meet or welcome the coming of the spirit ; " the last, "to escort the spirit on its departure." Before and after the service, the spirit does not reside in the tablet. As it is one of the prerogatives of the sovereigns of China " to sacrifice to or worship all spirits," he is called pâi shăn chih chû, "the host or entertainer of all spirits."

Dr. Morrison's account of the name shăn chû is not sufficiently complete, but it contains no inaccuracy, so far as it goes : " Shăn chû, a tablet in family temples with the name of the deceased inscribed on it. If he have held an official situation, the name of his office is inscribed before his own " (Dictionary I. i., p. 30).

NOTE G, p. 36.

This error does not surprise me so much as that the title-page of Regis' translation should say that the Yî is "*Antiquissimus Sinarum Liber.*" But this is due, I suppose, to the editor, and not to Regis, so difficult is it to free one's self from the entanglement of a blunder that has once obtained currency.

NOTE H, p. 39.

Professor Tiele (Religion of the Chinese, p. 28) says: " The twelfth century B.C. is the era of the establishment of the Châu dynasty, whose cultus we know from the book Châu Lî. Plath objects to the conception of the joint working of heaven and earth as a marriage, and describes the earth as a feudal prince. But the great power which they exert is called generation (sâng) and in the Yî King they are frequently represented as husband and wife, as father and mother. The same idea occurs also in the Shû King. See the passages cited by Plath

himself, ' Rel. der alten Chinesen,' pp. 35—38, and 73.
To treat this as a type of parental care is inappropriate.
The two original principles, Yang and Yin, which Plath
regards as the fruit of later philosophical reflection, make
their appearance as early as 1100 B.C. in the Châu Lî,
op. cit. vii. 3, and ix. 10, 11 ; and in the same work it is
not the chief vassal of the empire, but the principal wife
of the emperor, who is named after the earth. The
old and generally diffused myth of the marriage between
heaven and earth certainly lies at the foundation of
Chinese mythology also, though the philosophers afterwards disguised it past recognition."

I have thought it well to give the whole of Tiele's note.
When he says that it is not the chief vassal, but the
principal wife of the emperor, that is named after the
earth, he must intend to say that the earth is not named
after the chief vassal, but after the principal wife,—
referring to the phraseology " Hwang T'ien, Hâu T'û,"
of which there is an instance in the prayer quoted from
Dr. Edkins on p. 34, and translated by him, correctly,
" Imperial Heaven and Sovereign Earth." Hâu need not
be feminine any more than Hwang need be masculine.
This correction takes away the force of his argument in
adducing the phraseology. The idea he is insisting on
occurs indeed in the Shû, but only in the passages which I
have specially commented on at p. 30. He would hardly
have said that to treat the language in them as a type
of parental love is inappropriate, if he had known what
I have called attention to in a note on the same page, that
in the same sentence where "Heaven and Earth" is called
the father and mother of all creatures, the one sovereign
is called the father and mother of the people. Plath was
correct in saying that the joint working of heaven and
earth in the Yî was not to be regarded as the result of
their marriage. A marriage and its consequences by no
means covers the antinomy of the Yin and Yang.

NOTE I, p. 43.

These two sentences are the twenty-fourth and thirty-second of what is called "the Great Appendix (Section 1)." The former appears in P. Regis as—"Principia Yin Yang habent viam suam seu operandi ordinem certum modumque vel legem naturalem."—Dr. Medhurst (Theology of the Chinese, p. 114,) translated it by, "One male principle or (? and) one female principle of nature may be called the right course of things." Canon M'Clatchie has, "The revolving Darkness-Light is Reason." The second sentence appears in P. Regis as—"Quod non cadit sub mensuram modumque principiorum Yin, Yang, dicitur Chin (Shăn) Spiritus." Dr. Medhurst translated it by—"The inscrutable character of the male and female principle may be denominated Shăn, the mysterious." Canon M'Clatchie has, "That which is incomprehensible in the Darkness-Light (Yin-Yang) is God."

Strangely enough, the meaning found by Canon M'Clatchie is the same as that which I also find in it. He comes to his view, however, by mistranslating the character shăn, which means spirit and spiritual, and the view is incongruous on his system of interpretation. The rendering of shăn by Dr. Medhurst, mysterious, is only admissible when we bear in mind that behind the mysterious is the idea of spirit, spiritual.

NOTE K. p. 44.

So I must understand the title Hwang T'ien Shang Tî (皇天上帝) literally—"Sovereign Heaven, Supreme God." But the two pairs of characters cannot well be taken as binomial nouns in apposition, nor can we construe the first pair as performing the part of an adjective, and qualifying the second. The version which I have given is not contrary to Chinese usage.

When the Roman Catholic missionaries at Peking,
during the K'ang-hsî period (1662—1722), were disputing
among themselves about the meaning of the names T'ien
and Shang Tî, those on one side presented a memorial
to the emperor in Manchû, submitting their view that
the two names denote but one object,—the Supreme
Ruler, and that T'ien, singly or with attributives, was to
be understood of the place of Tî, employed, according
to Chinese usage, to avoid directly naming Him.   The
emperor caused their memorial to be translated into
Chinese, and published it in the imperial Gazette, with
a declaration of his own approval of their views.   See
Remusat's " Notices des Manuscrits," pp. 414, 415.

NOTE L, p. 57.

The Chinese character tsî $\left(祭\right)$ covers a much wider
space of meaning than our term sacrifice.   The account
of it in Morrison's Dictionary, Part i., taken mainly from
the K'ang-hsî dictionary, is—"To carry human affairs
before the gods (*i.e.* spirits).   That which is the medium
between, or brings together, men and gods.   To offer
flesh in the rites of worship ; to sacrifice with victims."
There is nothing in the K'ang-hsî corresponding to his
third sentence ; but I suppose Morrison took it from the
account of the character that is quoted from Hsü Shan's
dictionary, and which says that tsî is made up of two
ideagrams ;—one the primitive for spiritual beings (see
p. 11), and the other representing a right hand and a
piece of flesh.   Offerings of flesh must have been common
in religious worship when the character was formed.
The most general idea symbolised by it is—an offering
whereby communication and communion with spiritual
beings is effected.

II.

CONFUCIANISM: ITS WORSHIP OF THE DEAD, AND TEACHING ABOUT MAN. CONFUCIUS.

敦孝弟以重人倫

" Esteem most highly filial piety and brotherly submission, in order to give their due importance to the social relations." — *The K'ang-hsî Sacred Edict*, Precept I.

" Honour thy father and thy mother ; that thy days may be long in the land which the Lord thy God giveth thee."—*Fifth Commandment.*

II.

The worship of their forefathers by all the Chinese people.

1. THE first thing to be set forth in the present Lecture is the Confucian worship of ancestors. The former Lecture was occupied principally with the worship of God as performed by the sovereign of China for himself and as the representative of his people; the worship of his ancestors is also a part of the state ceremonial, but in performing this the sovereign does not stand alone;—the worship of their forefathers has always been the practice of all the Chinese people.

We found that a belief in one supreme and only God was coeval with the fathers and founders of the nation, and was testified to by the primitive written characters. The worship of God was, no doubt, the first, and for a time, probably, the only worship. By-and-by all nature was conceived to be a manifestation of God, and to be peopled with spirits superintend-

ing and controlling its different parts in subordination to Him. There grew up a worship
of these spirits in connexion with the worship
of God. The name of God was not given to
them, but honour was done to them as ministers
of God, and help might be sought from them
as mediators with Him. And it came about,
as we saw, that the worship of God and of these
spirits was all devolved on the Head of the
people. At the same time the recognition of
the one God was common to all. They knew
that in Him they " lived and moved and had
their being," and that His will should be the
rule of their lives. All derived from Him their
life and nature ; all owed to Him the duties of
obedience and reverence.

The philosopher Mencius says in one place,
that " though a man were wicked, yet if he
adjusted his thoughts, fasted, and bathed, he
might sacrifice to God."[1] The language shows
the value that Mencius attached to penitent
purification, and how he felt that all men had to
do with God. But the people were debarred from
the worship of Him. That was done for them
vicariously. Men, however, must worship, and as
they were cut off from worshipping God, there
remained for them the worship of their ancestors.

[1] Mencius, IV. ii. ch. 23.

Filial piety.—-The worship of parents a part of it.

2. According to Confucius, the worship of parents is part of the duty of filial piety. " The services," he said, " of love and reverence to parents when alive, and those of grief and sorrow for them when dead :—these completely discharge the fundamental duty of living men."[2] The fundamental duty of living men is filial piety, and among the services of grief and sorrow to parents when dead, the worship of them holds a prominent place. Confucius was expressing in these sentiments the tradition of his race. The character for filial piety, called hsiâo, is one of the primitive characters : used itself as a phonetic element, it is yet made up of two other primitives, the symbols or pictures of an old man and a son.[3] Thus the primary conception of filial piety was set forth by the picture of a son bearing up, or supporting, his father. But supporting and nourishing by no means exhaust the duty or virtue. Take a pretty full description of it from the sage.

[2] The Hsiâo King, ch. 18.

[3] Hsiâo (孝) = lâo (老, an old man) over tsze (子, a son).

" The service," said he, " which a filial son does
to his parents is as follows :—In his general
conduct to them, he manifests the utmost
reverence ; in his nourishing of them, his endeavour is to give them the utmost pleasure ;
when they are ill, he feels the greatest anxiety ;
in mourning for them (dead), he exhibits every
demonstration of grief ; in sacrificing to them,
he displays the utmost solemnity. When a son
is complete in these five things, (he may be
pronounced) able to serve his parents.

" He who (thus) serves his parents, in a high
situation will be free from pride ; in a low situation will be free from insubordination ; and
among his equals will not be quarrelsome. In
a high situation, pride leads to ruin ; in a low
situation, insubordination leads to punishment ;
among equals, quarrelsomeness leads to the
wielding of weapons. If those three things be
not put away, though a son every day contribute
beef, mutton, and pork to nourish his parents, he
is not filial."[1] With the sentiment in this last
sentence may be compared what Confucius says
in the Analects, that the reverence of parents
was necessary to distinguish our support of them
from that given to our horses and dogs.[2]

[1] The Hsiâo King, ch. 10.
[2] Analects, II. vii.

Filial piety and worship of Shun; and
subsequently down to the Châu
dynasty.—Living representatives of the
dead then employed.

3. It was in the account of the ancient Shun,
given in the Shû King, that we found the first
instances of religious worship addressed to God
and to the host of spirits. Shun's first appearance in the Shû is in connexion with the report
of his filial piety. It was that virtue which led
to his elevation to the throne; and we have in
the classic clear intimation that the worship of
ancestors was observed even in his time. He
asks his chief minister, to whom he should
commit the direction of his three (religious)
ceremonies,—the ceremonies, that is, in the
worship of the spirits of heaven, of earth, and
of men. One Po-î being recommended, he
appoints him in these words: "Ho! Po, you
must be the arranger in the Ancestral Temple.
Morning and night be reverent. Be upright, be
pure."[1] Thus the dignitary whom we may call
the minister of Religion at the court of Shun was
specially denominated the arranger in the Ancestral Temple. The ceremonies belonging to that
would require most of his time and attention.

[1] The Shû, II. i. 23.

Our information about the services in the ancestral temple increases, as might be expected, as time goes on. What Confucius said of them as practised by the founders of the Châu dynasty might have been said, I believe, from the time of Shun. Once every season worship was performed. "In spring and autumn," —and it might have been added in summer and winter—"they repaired and beautified the temple of their ancestors, set forth the vessels that had belonged to them, displayed their various robes, and presented the offerings of the several seasons." [2] The worshipper, as preliminary to the service, when it was confined to one ancestor, had to fast for two days, and to think of the person whom he was intending to honour,— where he had stood and sat, how he had smiled and spoken, what had been his cherished aims, pleasures, and delights ; and on the third day he would have a complete image of him in his mind's eye. Then on the day of the service, when he entered the temple, he would seem to see him in the shrine, and to hear him as he went about in the discharge of his worship.

There are in the Shih two odes descriptive of the worship of T'ang, the founder of the Shang

[2] Doctrine of the Mean, ch. 19.

dynasty (B.C. 1766—1122). I will read to you
one of them, written apparently by a member
of the royal House who had taken part in the
service :—

" O grand ! The drums, both large and for the hand,
    Complete in number, all in order stand :
    Their tones, though loud, harmoniously are blent,
    And rise to greet our ancestor's descent.

Him the great T'ang, of merit vast, our king
Asks by this music to descend, and bring
To us, the worshippers, the soothing sense
That he, the object of desire intense,
Is here. Deep are the sounds the drums emit ;
And now we hear the flutes, which shrilly fit
Into the diapason :—concord great,
Which the sonorous gem doth regulate !
Majestic is our king of T'ang's great line,
Whose instruments such qualities combine.

Large bells we hear, which with the drums have place,
While in the court the dancers move with grace.
Scions of ancient lines the service view,
Pleased and delighted, guests of goodness true.
Such service we received from former days,
Down from our sires who showed us virtue's ways,—
How to be meek and mild, from morn to night,
And reverently discharge our parts aright.

May T'ang accept the rites his son thus pays,
As round the winter comes, and autumn days ! "

In the Shû, in "The Speech at Kan," probably
a contemporaneous document of about 2194
B.C., the second sovereign of the Hsiâ dynasty

is leading his troops against a rebellious vassal, to inflict on him " the punishment appointed by Heaven." Having exhorted them to be valiant, he concludes by saying, "You who obey my orders shall be rewarded before (the spirits of) my ancestors, and you who disobey my orders shall be put to death before the altar of the spirit of the land." This seems to indicate that the ancient kings carried with them to the field the tablets of the spirits of their ancestors and of the spirit of the land, to be an omen of success, just as the army of Israel required on one occasion that the ark of God should be brought to the camp.

We conclude also from this passage that the spirit-tablets, of which I spoke in the former lecture, were in use at the commencement of the Hsiâ period, and I embrace the occasion which it presents to mention a strange innovation in this practice that took place during the period of Châu. The wooden tablet was discarded, and the departed ancestors were represented at the service by living relatives of the same surname, chosen according to certain rules. These took for the time the place of the dead, received the honours which were due to them, and were supposed to be possessed by their spirits. They ate and drank as those whom they personated would have done; accepted for them the homage rendered by their descendants, communicated their will to the principal worshipper, and pronounced on him and on his line their benediction, being assisted in this point by a mediating officer of prayer. This strange practice of using living relatives at the ancestral worship, instead of the wooden tablets, passed away with the dynasty in which it prevailed. I make but one other remark about it ;—strange as it was, it confirms my opinion that there was, and is, nothing of fetishism in the use of the spirit-tablet.

Further description of the filial piety and worship of the Châu kings.—Titles and worship carried back to ancestors.— Seasons of worship were family reunions.

4. The Shih abounds in pieces descriptive of the services in the ancestral temple of the Châu kings. There are others which may be denominated sacred songs of filial piety. This virtue is celebrated as the crowning attribute of the founders of the dynasty. Take as a specimen the following piece in praise of Wû, who heads the list of the actual sovereigns of his line :—

" Kings die in Châu, and others rise,
    And in their footsteps tread.

Three had there been, and all were wise,
    And still they ruled, though dead.
T'âi, Chî, and Wăn were all in heaven,
When Wû to follow them was given.

Yes, Wû to follow them was given.
    To imitate his sires,
And to obey the will of Heaven,
    He ardently desires.
This aim through all his course endured,
And this the people's trust secured.

Yes, Wû secured the people's faith,
    And gave to all the law
Of filial duty, which till death
    Shining in him they saw.
Such piety possessed his mind ;
Such pattern did he leave behind.

Thus the one man was Wû, the One,
    The king whom all did love.
They saw in him the pattern son ;
    Such sons to be they strove.
The filial aim in him bright shone;
In him were seen the dead and gone.

In Wû his sires were thus brought back.
    The kings that from him spring,
Continuing in his steps to walk,
    Upon themselves shall bring,
Through myriad years to Châu still given,
The blessing of impartial Heaven.

Ah ! yes, Heaven's blessing will descend,
    And men their names shall bless.
Thousands from Châu's remotest end
    Their praises shall express.
Their sway through myriad years shall last,
Nor helpers fail, strong friends and fast."

Besides the innovation of living representatives of the departed in the ancestral temple,
another alteration in the manner of the worship
was made by the famous legislator of the Châu
dynasty.   Confucius says in the Hsiâo: " Of all
the actions of man, there is none greater than
filial piety ; and in filial piety there is nothing
greater than the reverential awe of one's father.
In the reverential awe shown to one's father
there is nothing greater than making him the
correlate of Heaven.   The duke of Châu was
the one who first did this." [1]   That is, as the
text goes on to say, the duke of Châu associated
the remote ancestor of his line with the service
at the border altar to Heaven, and instituted
another great service to God, at which his father,
king Wăn, was the correlate or assessor.   Many
of the Chinese scholars, in explaining the
passage, say that Shun thought only of the
virtue of his ancestors, and did not associate
the spirits of any of them with the worship at
the border altar; that the kings of Hsiâ and
Yin were the first to do this with the founders
of their lines ; but that the honour was not extended to the father of the sovereign till the duke
of Châu.   This explanation of the language of
Confucius I am constrained to accept ; and it

---

[1] The Hsiâo, ch. ix.

gives us a glimpse of the earliest worship of God in the prehistoric time. He occupies His altar alone. No spirit-tablets of favoured and distinguished men are allowed upon it. The service has nothing to make us regard it as a feast or banquet. It was a tribute of homage and gratitude to the one Lord and Governor by the Head and representative of the Chinese people.

And the duke of Châu did more than give a place to the tablet of his father, on the altar of God. "He carried up the title of king to his grandfather and great-grandfather, and sacrificed to all the former dukes of the line with the ceremonies due to the Son of Heaven."[1] Such has been the rule in all subsequent dynasties. The emperors of the present Manchù dynasty have actually possessed the throne only since 1644, but the title is given to six others who preceded them as kings or chieftains of their Manchurian inheritance. These share with the sovereigns since 1644 in the worship, which is performed in the grand ancestral temple at the end of the year, while the more frequent worship in the first month of each season extends only to the grandfather of the first emperor. Their wives also have a part in the service,

---

[1] Doctrine of the Mean, ch. 18.

each pair of tablets being placed side by side in one shrine.

From what has been said, it will appear to you that those great seasonal occasions at the court of China have always been what we might call grand family reunions, where the dead and the living meet, eating and drinking together,— where the living worship the dead, and the dead bless the living. This appears very clearly in the following lines from a long ballad sung at the court of one of the marquises of Lû, of the seventh century B.C. :—

> " In autumn comes the autumnal rite,
>   With bulls, whose horns in summer bright
>   Were capped with care : [1]—one of them white,
>   For the great duke of Châu designed ;
>   One red, for all our princes shrined.
>   And see ! they place the goblet full,
>   In figure fashioned as a bull ;
>   The dishes of bamboo and wood ;
>   Sliced meat, roast pig, and pottage good,
>   And the large stand.   Below the hall
>   There wheel and move the dancers all ;
>   O filial prince, your sires will bless,
>   And grant you glorious success.
>   Long life and goodness they'll bestow
>   On you, to hold the state of Lû.

[1] The horns of the bulls were capped, to keep them from goring, and also to preserve them from injury. If they were in any way injured, they could not be used as victims.

6

And all the eastern land secure,
Like moon complete, like mountain sure.
No earthquake's shock, or flood's wild rage,
Shall e'er disturb your happy age ;
And with your aged nobles three,
Unbroken shall your friendship be,
In long and firm security." [1]

Prayers to the dead.

5. Of the prayers or addresses in the ancestral worship, the time will only permit me to
give three brief specimens. The two following
are from the statutes of the Ming dynasty :—" I
think of you, my sovereign ancestors, whose
glorious souls are in heaven. As from an overflowing fountain run the happy streams, such is
the connexion between you and your descendants. I, a distant descendant, having received
the appointment (from Heaven), look back and
offer this bright sacrifice to you, the honoured
ones from age to age, for hundreds of thousands
and myriads of years." And again : " Now
brightly manifested, now mysteriously hid, the
movements of the spirits are without trace ;
in their imperial chariots they wander about,
tranquil wherever they go. Their souls are in
heaven ; their tablets are in the rear apartment.
Their sons and grandsons remember them with

[1] The Shih, IV. ii., Ode 4.

filial thoughts untiring." To the same effect, and in nearly the same language, is a concluding prayer of the present dynasty, taken from a ritual published in 1826. "Now ye front us, (O Spirits,) and now 'ye pass by us, ascending and descending, unrestricted by conditions of place. The adytum behind is still and retired, very tranquil and felicitous. Your souls are in heaven; your tablets are in that apartment. For myriads of years will your descendants think of you with filial thoughts unwearied."

Something pleasing about filial worship, but it was injurious.

6. A recent writer who has carefully studied the ritualistic books of the Châu dynasty, has said : " It was supposed to be the glory of the early statesmen and sages to have correctly apprehended the natural feeling of filial duty, so as to make it an engine for the perfect government of the family, the state, and the empire. In the description given us of the intention of the sages we seem to lose sight of superstition, and to be in the presence of practices as harmless as some which flourish in Christian countries." [1] There is considerable truth in this representa-

[1] Rev. John Macintyre, in the *China Review*, VII. v. 249.

tion. The people, as I have already pointed out, being cut off from the worship of God for themselves, there remained for them the worship of their ancestors,[1] the only other channel that had been opened in the nation for the flow of religious feeling. The sages, therefore, dealt with filial duty so as to make a religion of it. It was not a religion capable of existing by itself, apart from the belief in and worship of the one God, the Lord and Governor; but it stood side by side with that higher worship, and the influence of it was injurious.

Ancestors became tutelary spirits.—Service of the duke of Châu.

7. The ancestors of the kings were exalted to the position of the tutelary spirits of the dynasty, and the ancestors of each family became its tutelary spirits. This result appears clearly in the passage on p. 81 from one of the praise-

[1] The following passage from the will of Napoleon III. sounds remarkably like a Chinese utterance :—" It is necessary to consider that from heaven on high those whom you have loved regard and protect you ;—it is the soul of my illustrious uncle that has always inspired and sustained me. The like will apply to my son, for he will always be worthy of his name. With regard to my son, let him be convinced that my heart and my soul remain with him."

songs of Lû. And it is even more remarkably shown in the fifth part of the Shû, in the book called "The Metal-bound Coffer." There the duke of Châu appears proposing to die in lieu of his brother who was dangerously ill, and whose life he considered more necessary to their infant dynasty than his own. To accomplish his object, he conducts a special service to his father, grandfather, and great-grandfather, and prays to them as having in heaven the charge of watching over the life of king Wû, and the interests of their line, begging that his own death may be accepted in substitution for that of Wû. We are told that the day after this prayer the king got better, while the duke of Châu continued to live and act as chief minister.

Defect of the system.—Case of Ch'ăng Î.— Has driven the masses to the Tâoists.

8. The ancestral worship thus tended to produce the superstition of tutelary spirits. And there was also a great defect attaching to it. It originated in the feudal time, when the king and the vassal lords, with their high nobles and great officers, all had their temples. The worship of their ancestors could be kept up by them ; but what provision was there for its maintenance among the masses of the people ?

When the feudal system passed away, the case was harder still. Ch'ǎng Î, a very distinguished scholar of our eleventh century, tells us that in his time most of the families of great officers, and other officers, neglected the worship of their ancestors and other traditional rites. They might be attentive to the support of their parents, but they failed in doing what was required of them for their ancestors. The state of things, he says, was very deplorable. He himself had a temple,—perhaps it was only a large shrine,—connected with his house, and furnished with the spirit-tablets of his ancestors. Before these, on the first day of each month, he set forth fresh offerings. He observed the seasonal services in the second month of each season. At the winter solstice he sacrificed to his remotest ancestor; in the beginning of spring, to his grandfather; and in the third month of autumn, to his father. On the anniversary of a death, he removed the tablet of the individual to the principal adytum of the temple, and there performed a special service; for the rites of the service of the dead ought to be observed more liberally than the duty of nourishing the living.[1]

This is an interesting account of the practice

[1] Taken from Chû Hsî's Hsiâo Hsio, Bk. 5, par. 6.

of an extraordinary man, though it may occur to us to doubt whether it was healthy for his mind to dwell so much with the dead. It was possible, however, for him, a man of culture and wealth, and latterly in an official position, to maintain his temple and keep all the days he mentions ; but such a thing is not possible for the common people. Unable to observe the ancestral worship as prescribed in the Confucian literature, finding it too cold and too exacting, they have thrown themselves into the arms of the Tâoists and Buddhists, becoming the victims especially of Tâoist superstition. It does not fall within my province to describe in this Lecture the actual ancestral worship that is, through the prevalence of Tâoism, a great feature in the social life of the country. Millions fancy that their dead, and other dead, are in a sort of purgatory, and will spite and injure them if they do not bring about their deliverance. The Tâoist professors fleece them in order to effect that object, and are wonderfully ingenious in finding occasions to wheedle or frighten their victims out of their money. Feeling, in itself good and admirable, is abused, and made to supply the wages of greediness and deceit.[1]

[1] See an Essay on ancestral worship, by the Rev. Dr. Yates, in Records of the General Conference of Protestant

Result of the teaching of filial piety.

9. The Chinese teaching of filial piety has done much to turn the hearts of the children back to their fathers, and to keep them attached to them and their ways. I will point out in my fourth lecture wherein I think it wrong and injurious; but numberless instances, well attested, of filial devotion could be added.[1] We are justified in looking on the long-continued existence and growth of the nation as a verification of the promise attached to our fifth commandment, " Honour thy father and mother, that thy days may be long in the land which Jehovah thy God giveth thee."

The worship of the departed great.

10. The worship of the departed great need not detain us long. The theory of it is given

Missionaries in China, held at Shanghai in May, 1877 (Shang-hâi, Presbyterian Mission Press). Dr. Yates' account of his subject is full and graphic ; he unfortunately sees only its dark side.

[1] Dr. Yates has had a different experience. " Of all the people," he says, " of whom we have any knowledge, the sons of the Chinese are most unfilial, disobedient to parents, and pertinacious in having their own way. The filial duties of a Chinese son are performed after the death of his parents." I am thankful I have not to endorse this representation.

in the last paragraph of the book called "The Laws of Sacrifice," in the "Record of Rites or Ceremonies." It is there said : "The rule observed by the sage kings in instituting sacrifices was this,—that those who had legislated for the people should be sacrificed to, also those who had died in the diligent discharge of their duties, those whose toils had established states, and those who had warded off, or given succour in, great calamities."

Then follows a list of ancient worthies, distinguished by such achievements, and the paragraph concludes : "As to the sun, moon, and constellations of the zodiac, they are looked up to by men with admiration ; and as to mountains, forests, rivers, and valleys, the people derive from them their material resources. It is only such beneficial services that give a place in the sacrificial canon." It was shown in the former Lecture that, in what is briefly called sacrificing to the hills and other material objects, the worship is really paid to the spirits presiding over them for the good of men under God. So it is in regard to the worship of the benefactors of the people in all the course of time. It is dominated by the idea of the one God, the Lord and Governor, with which the Chinese fathers started in their social state. This is very evident in the following verses at one of the border services of the Châu dynasty, addressed to Ch'î or Hâu-chî, to whom its kings traced their lineage, and whom they honoured besides as the father of husbandry. He is one of those worthies mentioned in the paragraph in "The Laws of Sacrifice," and it was said to him :—

> " O thou, accomplished, great Hâu-chî,
>   To thee alone 'twas given,
> To be, by what we owe to thee,
>   The correlate of Heaven.
>
> On all who dwell within our land
>   Grain-food didst thou bestow :
> 'Tis to thy wonder-working hand
>   This gracious boon we owe.
>
> God had the wheat and barley meant
>   To nourish all mankind :
> None would have fathomed His intent
>   But for thy guiding mind.
>
> Man's social duties thou didst show
>   To every tribe and state :
> From thee the social virtues flow
>   That stamp our land ' the Great.' "

In such worship of the departed great there is little to shock us. The memory of the just and the good is blessed all the world over. Every nation should keep its benefactors in remembrance, and men everywhere should honour the names of all of every nation who have ministered by their example and instructions to the advance and amelioration of our race. But to build temples to the dead; to present offerings to them; to invoke and expect their presence at the service; and to expect and pray for their help :—these are things that are not founded in reason and truth, and that encourage superstition instead of contributing to the healthy edifying of the mind and manners.

Imperial worship of such, and its evils.

There is in Peking the "Temple of the kings and emperors of different dynasties," and twice a year, in spring and autumn, the reigning sovereign visits it, and worships the spirits of the long line, and of the most noted of their ministers. The sacrificial canon of 1826 contains the names of about a hundred and ninety sovereigns, from Fû-hsî downwards. The roll is a wonderful testimony to the continuous occupancy of the throne of China, and there is much to nourish the pride and soothe the mind of the worshipper in the thought that when his line has passed away, there will yet be a tablet in that or a similar hall to his spirit. The members of the Board of Rites, and the reigning emperor, decide what former sovereigns shall be included in the canon, and what excluded from it. Such a name as that of the founder of the Ch'in dynasty, the burner of the classical books, and destroyer of the Confucian scholars, can never obtain a place ; but in general there is little regard paid to the moral and intellectual character of the different sovereigns. The second Manchû emperor, the famous sovereign of the K'ang-hsî period, declared that it was unseemly for men to discuss the characters of those who had occupied the throne, and whether they should be sacrificed to or not. The canon thus becomes a tribute to power and place, without regard to worth and virtue. So it is in the worship of the departed great by the emperor : you can conceive how liable the practice is to be abused, when it descends among the people.

Warning of Confucius.

I consider that Confucius uttered his protest against it, when he said, "For a man to sacrifice to a spirit which does not belong to him is (mere) flattery."[1] The term employed is that which represents the spirits of the deceased.

[1] Analects, II. 24.

That all should worship the spirits of their ancestors was an institution of his country, which the sage himself observed; but to go beyond the circle of one's family and worship was nothing but flattery, a thing unauthorized, and done with a mercenary aim.[1]

Had the worship of the spirits of the departed a good moral influence?

11. It is time that I should go on to our next topic, and I will only detain you from it while I ask, and endeavour to answer, the question,—Have we reason to think that the worship of the spirits which has been described had or has now a beneficial, a moral and religious influence? Of course, we smile at the idea of the service having power to bring the spirits to the tablets from wherever they are; but as the significance of the Chinese term, which has been accepted as meaning sacrifice, is the having communion and communication with, we can conceive the sincere worshipper striving to recall his fathers, and dwelling on their virtues, till he feels the glow of affection, and resolves to be good as they were. I have often talked with Chinese on the subject, but never got full and satisfactory answers to my

[1] See Note A.

inquiries. They would assert they were benefited by the worship, and then refer me to three classical passages. The first was the language of Confucius, " How abundantly do spiritual beings display their powers! They cause all men under heaven to fast and purify themselves, and put on their richest dresses to engage in their sacrifices. Then, like overflowing water, they seem to be over the heads, and on the right and left (of their worshippers)."[1]

The second was the account of the good king Wăn, in one of the pieces of the Shih :—

> " Wăn formed himself upon his sires,
>   Nor gave their spirits pain.
> Well pleased were they.   Next he inspires
>   His wife.   His brethren fain
> To follow there.   In every state
> The chiefs on his example wait.
>
> In palace see him,—bland, serene ;
>   In fane,—with rev'rent fear.
> Unseen by men, he still felt seen
>   By spirits always near.
> Unweariedly did he maintain
> His virtue pure, and free from stain."[2]

The third passage was also from the Shih, from a long and admirable piece in which an

[1] Doctrine of the Mean, ch. 16.
[2] The Shih, III. ii., Ode 6.

aged marquis of Wei admonishes himself to a virtuous and intelligent course.[1] It is more to the point, and speaks of the spirits generally, and not only as intercourse is sought with them in the temple. Thus it runs :—

> " When mingling with superior men,
>   In friendly intercourse, oh ! then
>   How mild your face ! what harmony !
>   All wrong and error, how you flee !
>   When in your chamber, 'neath its light,
>   Your conscience keep as pure and bright.
>   Say not, ' No one can see me here ;
>   The place is secret.' Be in fear.
>   The spirits come, but when and where
>   No one beforehand can declare.
>   The more we should not spirits slight,
>   But ever feel as in their sight."

Man is the creature of God.

12. The third topic will now receive our attention,—What the religion of China teaches concerning man, especially as to his nature, his duty, and his destiny.

You remember the prayers at a great solstitial service of the Ming dynasty, which I introduced in my former Lecture,—how it was said in them that all the numerous tribes of living beings are indebted to God for their beginning ; that it is He alone, the Lord, who is the true parent

[1] *Ibid.*, III. iii., Ode 2.

of all things ; that He made heaven and earth
and men. Most of us were acquainted, I suppose,
at one time, with what is called " The First
Catechism," by Dr. Watts. The first question
in it is—" Can you tell me, child, who made
you ? " A Chinese child, familiar with those
prayers, would be likely to answer in the very
words of Dr. Watts, " The great God who made
heaven and earth." And the answer would be
according to the testimony of some of the oldest
Chinese documents. " Heaven gives birth to
the people,"[1] said Chung-hui, a minister of the
great T'ang, in the eighteenth century B.C.; and
the same sentiment is repeated in a poem of
the ninth century B.C.,—" Heaven gives birth
to mankind."[2] That man is the creature of
Heaven, or God, therefore, is a tenet of the
religion of China.

The most intelligent of all creatures.

In a passage which I adduced from the Shû
it is said that " man is the most intelligent of all
creatures."[3] If we ask what there is peculiar
in the constitution of man that gives him this

[1] The Shû, IV. ii. 2.
[2] The Shih, III. iii., Ode 6.
[3] The Shû, V. i., sect. 1. See p. 30.

superior intelligence, these ancient writings do not tell us. Mencius indeed says that " that whereby man differs from the lower animals is but small, and that the majority of people cast it away, while superior men preserve it ; " but, without pausing to define the differentiating character- istic, he goes on to specify the ancient Shun as one of the superior men. " Shun," he says, " clearly understood the (natures of) things, and marked the relations of men. He walked along the path of benevolence and righteousness, not needing to pursue it as by an effort."[1] The philosopher was not thinking metaphysically of the difference between men and animals, but wished to commend the cultivation of moral qualities to his hearers ; and hence Châo Ch'î of our second century, the great commentator on his works, says that the difference in question is " simply the interval between the knowledge of righteousness and the want of that know- ledge." This interval is indeed great, but it appears that the ancient Chinese held popularly that man is " the most intelligent of all creatures," just as we do when we say of some remarkable for their depravity that they put themselves below the level of the brutes.

[1] Mencius, IV. ii. 19.

The duty required of man is compliance with his moral nature.

13. On the duty required by God from this most intelligent of His creatures, and the way in which man was enabled, to fulfil it, we have the following statements. Thus spake T‘ang, whose name must by this time be familiar to your ears: " The great God has conferred (even) on the inferior people a moral sense, compliance with which would show their nature invariably right. To make them tranquilly pursue the course which it would indicate is the work of the sovereign."[1] To the same effect is what we read in the Shih, in a piece, referred to a little ago, of the ninth century B.C. : " Heaven, in giving birth to mankind, to every faculty and relationship annexed its laws. The people possess this normal nature, and they (consequently) love its normal virtue."[2] Thus every faculty of man has its function to fulfil, every relationship its duty to be discharged. The function and the duty are the laws which man has to observe. This is the normal nature conferred by Heaven, the moral sense, compliance with which would show men's conduct invariably

[1] The Shû, IV. iii. 2.
[2] The Shih, III. iii., Ode 6.

right. This moral sense constitutes man in his various relations " a law to himself."

Kings and sages appointed to rule and guide men to fulfil their duty.

14. But men need guidance and help in the use of their normal nature ; and T'ang's idea was that to define the course of duty and assist men to keep it was the work of the sovereign. The editors of the imperial edition of the Shû that appeared in 1730 pause at this point in the classic to express their admiration of T'ang. He was the first, they say, to bring out clearly the doctrine of human nature. It was contained in utterances of the more ancient Shun to which they refer, but only darkly. T'ang is worthy of their praise. Let it be borne in mind that he ascended the throne of China two hundred years before Moses was born according to our common chronology, and forty-four years earlier than that event according to the chronology of Dr. Hales. How grandly he speaks of our nature as given by God ! How nobly he conceived of the work of the sovereign !

His notion, indeed, of that work was pitched too high, though it has ruled ever since in the literature of China. It is the duty of the

sovereign to rule for the good of the people;
and when he has ceased to do so, he has for-
feited his title to the throne. Mencius formulated the doctrine in very striking language
when he said that "the people are the most
important element in a nation, and the ruler is
the lightest."[1]   But all sovereigns cannot be
expected to teach and guide the people.   They
are in the position of authority, but they may
not have either the moral superiority or the
intellectual ability that would fit them to realize
T'ang's ideal.   His theory was expanded, and
a new factor introduced, which we find stated
by king Wû, the first of the Châu kings, in
these words: "Heaven, to help the inferior
people, made for them rulers, and made for them
instructors, who should be assisting to God, and
help to secure tranquillity throughout the realm."[2]
This idea as to instructors, though not fully
enunciated by T'ang, was not beyond the range
of his thoughts. "I, the little child," said he,
"charged with the decree of Heaven, and its
bright terrors, did not dare to forgive (the
criminal).   I presumed to use a dark-coloured
victim bull, and, making clear announcement to
the spiritual sovereign in the high heavens,"—or.

[1] Mencius, VII. ii., ch. 14.
[2] The Shû, V., sect. i. 7.

as Confucius quotes the passage, "to the great and sovereign God,"—requested leave to deal with the ruler of Hsiâ as a criminal. Then I sought for the great sage, with whom I might unite my strength, to request the favour of Heaven for you, my multitudes."[1]

Thus the religion of China teaches that God made men, and endowed them with a good nature intended to lead them invariably right ; and to secure this result, He further appointed for them kings and wise men to rule and instruct them. Instruction to promote their virtue, and government to secure their happiness :—these were what Heaven made provision for in behalf of mankind.

Man's moral feebleness makes this necessary. —View of Confucius and Mencius.

15. But why was it necessary to make such provision for those who were furnished with so good a nature? " Heaven," it was said to T'ang by his minister Chung-hui, " Heaven gives birth to the people with (such) desires, that without a ruler they must fall into all disorders ; and Heaven again gives birth to the man of intelligence to regulate them." Man with his moral

[1] The Shû, IV. iii. 2 ; and Analects, XX. 1.

sense is yet in danger of going astray, is sure to
go astray. Nearly five hundred years before
T'ang, the same truth had been indicated by
Shun, when, as related in the Shû, he said to
his chief minister, " The mind of man is restless,
prone (to err) ; its affinity to what is right is
small. Be discriminating, be uniform (in pursuing what is right), that you may sincerely
hold fast the Mean."[1]   The same thing appears
later on in the first stanza of a remarkable piece
in the Shih, where king Wăn of Châu is introduced as warning the last sovereign of the
Shang dynasty, and saying to him,

> " How great is God, who ruleth men below !
>   In awful terrors now arrayed,
> His dealings seem a recklessness to show,
>   From which we shuddering shrink, dismayed.
> But men at first from Heaven their being drew,
>   With nature liable to change.
> All hearts in infancy are good and true,
>   But time and things those hearts derange."[2]

Such passages seem to teach a doctrine concerning human nature, not inconsistent with the
teaching of our Christian scriptures.   They seem
to teach this ; and I believe they do teach it.
For the full exposition of the Chinese view,
however, we must descend to the writings of

[1] The Shû, II. ii. 2.
[2] The Shih, III. iii., Ode 1.

Mencius, between thirteen and fourteen centuries after T'ang. Confucius had said that
" man is born for uprightness ; and that, if one
be without uprightness, and yet live, his escape
(from death) is the result of mere good fortune."[1]
Mencius, as his manner was, gave his opinion
more distinctly and roundly. " Man's nature is
good," he said. " The tendency of man's nature
to good is like the tendency of water to flow
downwards."[2] But he explained these statements, saying, " From the feelings proper to it,
we see that our nature is constituted for the
practice of what is good. This is what I mean
in saying that the nature is good. If men do
what is not good, the blame cannot be imputed
to their natural powers."[3] Few who consider
the subject without prejudice will object to this
view of Mencius. In fact, that philosopher, born
rather more than two thousand years before
bishop Butler, developed a theory of human
nature in which he anticipated every important
point insisted on by the Christian prelate. He
admitted, as Chung-hui had done, that man was
prone to go astray, and could not be safely left
to himself. By wrong-doing men were violating
the law of their nature, formed for goodness ;

[1] Analects, VI. xvii.
[2] Mencius, VI. i., ch. 1, 2. [3] *Ibid.,* ch. 6.

they must " seek for their lost heart," and then
keep it by following the example and obeying
the maxims of the sages. His analysis of the
constituents of humanity was correct. When
he came to speak of how men fall short in
their conduct of the ideal which it suggests, and
how they are to regain and keep that ideal, his
teaching was defective.

**The course of human duty confined to the
five constituent relationships of society.**

16. What now is the course of human duty as
laid down by the sages raised up by Heaven for
the purpose? In answering this question, I will
use the words of a Chinese writer of the last
century. In the year 1670 there was issued in
China what is known as the K'ang-hsî Sacred
Edict, containing sixteen precepts, by the
second emperor of the present dynasty, for
the instruction of the people. An amplifica-
tion of the precepts was published by his
successor, and portions of this are read and
explained twice a month all over the empire,
approaching more to our idea of sermons than
anything else in Confucianism. The first precept enjoins filial piety. This is the first and
greatest of the commandments in China. The
seventh is, " Discountenance and put away

strange principles in order to exalt the correct doctrine." Wang Yû-po, a very able para phrast, says on this : " Here is man, with his head towards heaven, and his feet planted on the earth, in the midst of all other existing things. He is endowed with the principle of rectitude all complete, and outside him there are the requirements of duty in his lot;—what is there wonderful and rare that he has to attend to? There are the relations of ruler and subject, father and son, husband and wife, elder brother and younger, friend and friend, and the duties severally belonging to them;— no one, intelligent or stupid, can dispense with these for a single day. If besides these, be- yond your proper lot, you go about to seek for some refined and mysterious dogmas, and to engage in strange and marvellous perfor- mances, you will show yourselves to be very bad men."

Such, then, is the whole duty of man in the religion of China, as expounded by the Chinese themselves. What the sages have taught are the duties binding on men in society. The scheme says nothing about men's duty to God. It is true that man's nature and the consti- tution of society are from Him, and that a performance of the duties belonging to the five relationships is obedience to His will ; but the duties are enforced without any immediate reference to God.   Our Christian catechisms put the matter differently.   The idea of God stands foremost in them : " Man's chief end is to glorify Him."   In the teaching of the Chinese religion, man's duty to God is left to take care of itself.

The five constituent relationships of society are mentioned in the canon of Shun in connexion with his appointment of a minister of Instruction.   Mencius refers to the passage in the Shû, and amplifies it, saying, " To men there belongs the way (in which they should go) ; and if they are well fed, warmly clad, and comfortably lodged, without being taught (at the same time), they become almost like the beasts.   This also was a subject of anxious solicitude to the sage (Shun), and he appointed Hsieh to be minister of Instruction, and to teach the relations of humanity,—how between father and son there should be affection ; between ruler and subject righteousness ; between husband and wife attention to their separate functions ; between old and young a proper distinction ; and between friend and friend fidelity."[1]

[1] Mencius, III. i., ch. 4.

Relationships of friend to friend and
    of husband and wife. — Position of
    woman.

17. I do not know any other scheme of society
which gives so prominent a place to friendship ;
and what is found in Chinese moralists on the
subject is of a noble character. The end of
friendship should be mutual helpfulness, and
especially the promotion of virtue. The separate
functions of husband and wife are—the direction
of all affairs outside the family by the husband, and of all matters inside by the wife,—
the leading of the husband, and the following
of the wife. I do not see that fault can be
found with this account of the duties of
husband and wife ; but as social life in China
becomes more like our social life in the west,
it will be found difficult to confine the wife's
attention entirely to her household affairs.
Even now I have often found the strong-
minded wife the regulator of things outside
as well as inside the family. And nominally
at least, during the minority of the present
emperor, as was the case also during that of
his predecessor, the government has been in the
hand of an empress-dowager and the empress-
mother. The condition of woman in China,

however, has always been inferior to that of man ; its religion does not look upon her with an equal eye. It is not till the wife becomes a mother—the mother of a son, that she takes a place in the family and the temple, on a level with her husband.

Historical view of the position of woman.—
Infanticide and foot-binding.

18. There are two common Chinese characters with the signification of wife. The older, and which is also a primitive belonging to the pre-historic time, is called ch'î, and denotes " the woman who is the mate or equal."[1] That this was the most ancient designation of a wife is satisfactory, and would have been entirely so but for our having among the primitive characters one called ch'ieh, and denoting a concubine.[2] Neither the primitive characters of China nor its written documents disclose to us a state of society in which the man had, or ought to have, only one sharer of his bed. The concubine was

[1] Ch'î (妻), composed of 女, a female, and another primitive, meaning—on a level with.

[2] Chieh (妾). The lower part of this is also 女, a female ; the upper is not fully ascertained.

inferior to the wife, and I do not know that we should call the system that prevailed by the name of polygamy ; but all Chinese history testifies to the evils springing from it.

In the "Canon of Yâo," the first document of the Shû King, the sage Yâo gives his two daughters in marriage at the same time to the sage Shun, as an experiment by which he might know whether Shun were fit to occupy his own place on the throne. Subsequently, as related also in the Shû, the ruin of both the dynasties of Hsiâ and Shang is occasioned by the wickedness of the concubines of their last monarchs. The Book of Poetry affords us many peeps into the domestic life at the court of king Wăn, the founder of the line of Châu, and subsequently at many of the feudal courts. T'âi-sze, Wăn's queen, is the theme of many pieces, and one of her noblest qualities is her freedom from jealousy, and her complacency even in the well-filled harem of her lord. Many will think that the force of degradation could no farther go.

There is a fine poem of the ninth century B.C. on the completion of a palace by king Hsüan.[1] The author augurs for the king all happiness in it ; and anticipating in the last two

[1] The Shih, II. vi., Ode 5.

stanzas the birth of sons and daughters, he thus
sings about them :—

" Sons shall be his,—on couches lulled to rest.
    The little ones, enrobed, with sceptres play ;
Their infant cries are loud as stern behest ;
    Their knees the vermeil covers shall display.
As king hereafter one shall be addressed ;
    The rest, as princes, in our states shall sway.

And daughters also to him shall be born.
    They shall be placed upon the ground to sleep ;
Their playthings tiles, their dress the simplest worn ;
    Their part alike from good and ill to keep.
And ne'er their parents' hearts to cause to mourn ;
    To cook the food, and spirit-malt to steep."

Dr. Morrison understood the line, " Their part
alike from good and ill to keep," as saying that
the daughters would be "incapable either of evil
or good,"[1] but the sentiment is not so extreme as
that.   It is simply this,—that a woman ought
to have no mind of her own, and not to take
the initiative either in good or ill.   In one piece
a bride is compared to a dove, but not because
of its gentleness and beauty, but because of its
quietness and stupidity.[2]   A stanza in a third
poem dilates on the evils caused by "a wise
woman," in terms which I do not care to quote."[3]

[1] See his Dictionary, I. i., p. 601.
[2] The Shih, I. ii., Ode 1.
[3] *Ibid.*, III. iii., Ode 10.

Infanticide has been charged against the Chinese, as showing their want of natural affection; and though it does not exist to the extent that has sometimes been represented, it meets you in most parts of the empire, and is owing mainly to the poverty of the people. The reason why I refer to it is because the victims of the unnatural practice are almost invariably girls. Woman certainly has no occasion to bless the religion of China. Both Confucius and Mencius were distinguished for their devotion to their mothers, and neither of them is open to the charge of having added a concubine to his wife; but their married life does not appear to have been very happy, and no generous sentiment tending to the amelioration of the social position of woman ever came from either.

The low opinion entertained of woman in China may be considered to have found its strongest expression between nine hundred and a thousand years ago, when the custom of binding and cramping the feet of girls commenced. I once saw a notice condemnatory of it in the Mohammedan mosque at Canton. It was a sin, the placard said, against the Supreme Lord, interfering with and disfiguring His handiwork; and Mohammedanism sternly forbade it. I never succeeded in warming a Chinese father to enthusiasm against the practice.[1] It is to the honour of the second emperor of the present dynasty that he prepared an edict commanding its suppression. The representations of his ministers about the opposition which it would encounter, however, made him withdraw it. Among the most furious in the outcry against it would have been the women themselves. So powerful is the dominion of fashion and habit !

Confucianism says nothing explicitly about the state of man after death.

19. The Confucian religion gives no explicit utterances on the state of man after death. It holds, and has always held, that, though dis-embodied, he continues to live on ; but it says very little, and nothing definite, as to the conditions of his future existence.

[1] In his "View of China for Philological Purposes," p. 28, Dr. Morrison quotes one account of the origin of this practice, under the date A.D. 916 ; but the Chinese writer prefaces his narrative with the statement that " it is not known when the bow (*i.e.* small) foot of females was introduced." Dr. Williams, (Middle Kingdom, II. p. 28,) mentions three different accounts of its origin ; but does not say which is the most correct. This is a point worth the attention of some Sinologue, who has the means of investigating it.

Classical testimonies.

20. I have already quoted in this Lecture[1] an ode of the Shih which says that " T'âi, Chî, and Wăn," three ancestors of the kings of Châu, "were all in heaven;" and I have also referred to the case of the duke of Châu, when he prayed to those same three, and asked that they would get his death accepted in lieu of that of his sick brother whose continued life was more important than his own to the interests of the kingdom.[2] Other pieces of the Shih are available to prove the ancient belief in the continued existence of the dead. In one of the books of the Shû, also, belonging to the fourteenth century B.C., king Pan-kăng, irritated by the opposition of the wealthy and powerful Houses to his measures, threatens them with calamities to be sent down by his ancestor, T'ang the Successful. He tells his ministers that their ancestors and fathers, who had loyally served his predecessors, were now urgently entreating T'ang to punish their descendants. Not only, therefore, did good sovereigns continue to have a happy existence in heaven, but their good ministers shared their happiness with them, and were round about them, as they had been

[1] See p. 78. [2] Page 85.

8

on earth, and took an interest in the progress
of the concerns which had occupied them during
their lifetime. Indeed, the two forms of worship, the origin of which I have traced to the
prehistoric time—the worship of God and the
worship of the departed—supposed the independent existence of spirits and the possibility
of communion with them at the services appointed in their honour. In the three prayers
which I adduced from those used in the imperial
ancestral temple it is said to the worshipped
dead, "Your souls are in heaven."[1]

That God is no idle occupant of His throne is
taught in a multitude of passages in the ancient
books. The words of the young king Ch'ăng,
in the twelfth century B.C., are of general
application :—

> " With reverence I will go
>   Where duty's path is plain.
> Heaven's will I clearly know ;
>   Its favour to retain
> Is hard ;—let me not say
>   ' Heaven is remote on high,
> Nor notices men's way.'
>   There in the starlit sky
> It round about us moves,
>   Inspecting all we do,
> And daily disapproves
>   What is not just and true."[2]

[1] Pp. 82, 83.   [2] The Shih, IV. i., Pt. 3, Ode 3.

In illustration of this point I will quote but one more passage; from one of the appendices to the Yî King, by Confucius.[1] "The family," it says, "that accumulates goodness is sure to have superabundant happiness; the family that accumulates evil is sure to have superabundant misery."

It may appear that this is descriptive only of Heaven's complacency in the good, and anger at the bad, and of retribution simply in time; and that, though we find rewards and dignity for the good after death, nothing is said of any punishment of the bad. So it is; and I have intimated my opinion that the system of ancestral worship prevented the development of the idea of future retribution.[2] The tyrant-oppressor might have his tablet in the temple, and his spirit be feasted and prayed to as much as if he had been a great benefactor of the people. One of the finest poems in the Shih is a prayer by king Hsüan of the ninth century B.C. in a time of excessive drought. He prays to his parents for succour, though his father had been notoriously worthless and wicked. Endeavours have been made to explain away the simple text, probably from a wish to avoid its seeming to give honour to one so undeserving of it.[3]

[1] The Yî, App. 7, par. 41. [2] Page 92.
[3] The Shih, III. iii., Ode 4, St. 4.

More modern view, that retribution takes place in time.

21. I have selected the illustration from the seventh appendix to the Yî, because it speaks of the issues of good and evil in the history of a family, and so far extends the theory of retribution into the future, just as our second commandment does ; but it is still the future of time. This view did not take definite shape until about the era of Confucius. The first distinct statement of it that I can call to mind was in 535 B.C., by a minister of Lû, on his death-bed. Giving orders that his son and another scion of his clan should become disciples of Confucius, who was then attracting the public notice, he referred to several ancestors of the sage, and said that in him was about to be verified the frequent saying of an eminent statesman, that " If a wise and good man do not get distinguished in his own time, there is sure to be among his posterity some one of vast intelligence." [1] This is the form in which the doctrine of future retribution is now generally spoken of by Chinese scholars. Virtue and vice have their appropriate issues, if not in the

[1] See the Tso Chwan, under the seventh year of duke Ch'âo.

experience of the individual, certainly in that of his posterity.

Four utterances of Confucius on the subject.

22. We need not be surprised that the old religion of China should speak thus indefinitely about the future state of man. Let us be thankful rather that it recognizes, as it does, his continued existence after death, and the ascent of the spirits or souls of the good to heaven. By the time of Confucius, however,—say in the fifth century B.C.,—men had come to wish for information more definite and minute. He himself avoided speaking on four subjects: extraordinary things; feats of strength; rebellious disorder; and spirits.[1] But he could not prevent his disciples from questioning him about them. It was not, after all, much that they learned from him, but I will close this division of my Lecture by relating it.

The first of his utterances is well known. Chî Lû, one of the foremost of his disciples, asked him once about the service of the spirits (of the dead), and he replied, "While you are not able to serve men (alive), how can you serve their spirits?" The disciple went on, "I venture

[1] Analects, VII. xx.

to ask about death;" and he was answered, "While you do not know life, how can you know about death?"[1]   Different views have been taken of these replies.   Some find a profound meaning in them; others merely the sage's avoiding unprofitable subjects.   This latter view seems the more correct.

The occasion of the second utterance of Confucius was the question of Tsze-kung, another distinguished follower, who asked him whether the dead had knowledge or not of the services rendered to them.   The master replied, "If I were to say the dead have such knowledge, I am afraid that filial sons and dutiful grandsons would injure their substance in paying the last offices to the departed; and if I were to say that the dead have not such knowledge, I am afraid that unfilial sons would leave their parents unburied.   You need not wish to learn whether the dead have such knowledge or not.   There is no present urgency about the point.   Hereafter you will know it for yourself."[2]   The former utterance was from the Confucian Analects, and may be accepted as genuine.   This other is from the "Narratives of the School," the authority of which does not stand so high.

[1] Analects, XI. xi.
[2] The Chiâ Yü, II., Art 1.

I would hope that, though generally accepted by the Chinese, it is not genuine. It gives us no information, and certainly was not the teaching proper to a sage.

The third utterance is from the ninth book of the " Record of Rites," where Confucius is conversing with Yen Yen. He says, " (By-and-by), when one died, (his friends) went on the housetop, and cried out to him by name to come back, (wishing his soul to return). Afterwards they set forth by the corpse rice uncooked and crude, and pieces of roasted flesh. Thus they looked up to heaven (where the soul was gone), and buried (the body) in the earth. The body and animal soul descend, while the intelligent spirit is on high. Hence the dead are laid with their heads to the north, and the living stand facing the south. In all these matters they followed (the ways at) the beginning (of funeral and sacrificial rites).[1] The practice of going on the

---

[1] See the Lî Yun, Part i. 7. The text, it is supposed by many, contains a Tâoistic element, surreptitiously introduced by the compilers under the Han dynasty. Portions, including this paragraph, are thrown out of some editions. The name of "the intelligent spirit" is literally, "the knowing breath." The character is ch'î, and not shăn, "the breath" being used like the Hebrew ruach and the Latin spiritus. A famous commentator, Ch'ăn Hsiang-tâo, says, "The body and animal soul are

top of the house, when a death has taken place
in it, and shouting to the deceased to come back,
is still observed in China.   But the importance
of the passage, if it be authentic, about which
there is some doubt, is the testimony which it
gives as to the ancient belief in the separation
of the soul and body at death, and the continued
existence of the former on high.

Much to the same effect is the fourth utterance, found also in the " Record of Rites," in
the twenty-fourth book.   There the disciple Tsâi
Wo says, " I have heard the names kwei and
shân, but I do not know what they mean."
Confucius said, " The (intelligent) spirit is of
the shân nature, and shows that in fullest
measure ; the animal soul is of the kwei
nature, and shows that in fullest measure.   It is
the union of kwei and shân that forms the
highest exhibition of doctrine.

" All the living must die, and, dying, return
to the ground ; this is what is called kwei.

extinguished, and nothing of them remains.   But the
intelligent soul continues to be moved and to move, and
always is."   Compare a passage in Professor Max Müller's
" Philosophy of Mythology," p. 359, *et seq.*, beginning,
" When man wished for the first time to grasp and express
a distinction between the body, and something else within
him distinct from the body, an easy name that suggested
itself was *breath.*"

The bones and flesh moulder away below, and, hidden away, become the earth of the fields. But the spirit issues forth, and is displayed on high in a condition of glorious brightness. The vapours and odours which produce a feeling of sadness (and arise from the decay of their bodies) are the subtle essences of animals, and (also) a manifestation of the shân nature." [1]

You may think that in this passage, attributed to Confucius, counsel is darkened by a multitude of words without knowledge. It is not for me, however, to attempt an elucidation of every part of it. I have adduced it to show how he held that, while man's body crumbles and returns to the dust at death, the liberated spirit, "the breath," [2] as he phrases it, ascends to a brighter state. The body and the animal soul cease to be, excepting as they may mingle with the dust of matter, but the intelligent soul or the spirit lives on in the bright heaven. Of its condition there the Confucian religion says nothing ; nor does it say how it can come from heaven, when sacrificed to, and communicate and commune with its sincere worshippers from the spirit-

[1] See Note B.

[2] Is there not in this term a groping after what we are told in Genesis ii. 7, " And the Lord God formed man of the dust of the ground, and breathed into his nostrils the breath of life ; and man became a living soul "?

tablet. That religion teaches the existence of the soul after death, but nothing of the character of that existence; and so it does not fan the flame of faith or hope in regard to the future in its friends and adherents.

Conclusions.

23. I must now leave the subject of the most ancient or state religion of China,—what I have called Confucianism,—and give a brief account of Confucius himself. I have described that religion from three points of view,—what it teaches concerning God, concerning spirits, and concerning man. I have endeavoured to trace the fundamental ideas of it on these subjects from the earliest, even from prehistoric, time down to the present day, and to show how the worship of God has been a matter of state ceremonial, and the worship of ancestors has extended to all the people. I am sorry that sometimes I may have seemed to be debating and arguing, and not simply relating and describing. There is no help for this. There are not any subjects, political, historical, or religious, even here in Europe, however long and extensively they have been discussed, on which there is an universal agreement of opinion : it is no wonder that different views should be

entertained about the religion of China, a subject of comparatively recent study. I have done what I could to form my own opinions after sufficient research, and to express them to you clearly and dispassionately, avoiding as much as I could expressions of praise or blame. Of the value of the old religion of China, I shall have to speak when I come to compare it, in my concluding Lecture, with Christianity. Let me now direct your attention to Confucius, lest my account of Confucianism should be thought like the play of *Hamlet* with Hamlet himself left out.

It has become, I have no doubt, sufficiently clear to you that both the views of Confucianism which I mentioned at the commencement of my former Lecture are erroneous. China does not owe its national religion to Confucius. He received it, as did others, from prehistoric time, both in its twofold worship and in its rules of social duty; and on this point I need say nothing more. And if Confucius did not originate the religion of his country, neither did he discountenance it, or alter it in any sensible degree. I have quoted his words freely, to illustrate the ideas and practices of the more ancient sages, and we have found them pervaded by religious sentiment. He taught morality,

but not a morality without reference to the
will of God. He taught ceremonialism, but
not for the sake of the ceremony merely. His
formalism did not content itself with the
outward observance of established rites. These
statements will receive further illustration as I
proceed to give you in brief compass a sketch
of the life and character of the man.[1]

Sketch of the life of Confucius.—His birth in B.C. 551 to his marriage.

24. Confucius,—that is, K'ung-foo-tsze,
"the master K'ung,"—was born in the year 551
B.C., in Lû, one of the feudal states, and covering
a considerable part of what is now the province
of Shan-tung. His father, known to us by the
name of Liang-ho, and an officer remarkable
for his strength, bravery, and skill, was over
seventy years old when the future sage was
born.[2] Their lineage was as distinguished as any
in China could be, for the K'ung family traced
its line to the sovereigns of the Shang dynasty,
and back from them, among the mists of hardly
discernible antiquity, to the mythical Hwang Tî,

[1] See Note C.

[2] See the prolegomena to the Chinese Classics, Vol. I.,
for a fuller account of Confucius, and reference to the
authorities for statements here.

in the twenty-eighth century B.C.   The old
soldier died when Confucius was in his third
year, and his mother, in bringing him up, had to
struggle with poverty.   At a later time, when
people were surprised at the many things he
could do, he said, " When I was young, my
condition was low, and I acquired my ability
in many things ; but they were mean matters."
We know little of his youth.   Accounts describe
the boy as fond of playing at the arrangement
of sacrificial vessels, and at postures of ceremony.
He tells us himself that at fifteen his mind was
set on learning.

From his marriage to his visiting the court of Châu, B.C. 533—517.

25. At nineteen he married, and his only son,
Lî, was born the year after.   About the same
time we find him in charge, but whether in the
service of the state, or merely of one of the
ministers, cannot be determined,—in charge of
some stores of grain, and subsequently of the
public fields.   Mencius refers to those employ-
ments in illustration of his doctrine that the
superior man may at times take office simply
for the relief of his poverty, but must in such a
case confine himself to places of small emolu-
ment, and aim at nothing but the discharge of

their humble duties.   This was what Confucius did.

In his twenty-second year he commenced his labours as a teacher, and his house became a resort—not for schoolboys, but for young and inquiring spirits who wished to increase their knowledge of the history and doctrines of the past.   However small the fee that was given, he never refused his instructions ;   but he did require an ardent desire for improvement and some degree of capacity.

His mother died in the year B.C. 528, and he mourned for her with the bitterest grief.   Having raised the coffin of his father from where it had been laid more than twenty years before, he had it conveyed, along with that of his mother, to the place where the K'ungs had first found refuge in Lû, and buried the two in the same grave.   To mark the spot, he employed some of his disciples to raise a mound over it ; and when told that this had fallen down through a sudden storm of rain, he burst into tears.

When the period of mourning for his mother was concluded, he remained in Lû for ten more years, pursuing his own literary researches, studying antiquities and music, and guiding the studies of others.   The chief men of the state were gradually becoming aware that a great man had risen among them ; and in B.C. 517, one of its principal ministers, as I have already related,[1] gave orders on his death-bed that his son, and another member of their clan, should enter the Confucian school. Such pupils increased its reputation in the country, and also enlarged the master's means. That same year he was able to visit the capital, and make fuller inquiries than he could do at a distance into the ceremonies and rules of the founders of the Châu dynasty. There also he is said to have met with Lâo-tsze, the father of Tâoism, and to have had various conversations with him. I may refer to these in my next Lecture. By the end of the year he was back in Lû, and resumed his work of teaching. His fame was greatly increased, and disciples came to him from all quarters, till their number amounted to thousands. We are not to think of them as forming a community, and living together. We find, indeed, the master after this always moving amid a company of admiring followers, but the greater number must have had their proper avocations and ways of living, and would only repair to him when they wished specially to ask his counsel.

In the year B.C. 516, there were great troubles

[1] Page 116.

in Lû, and the marquis, worsted in a struggle with the three great families or clans of the state, fled from it to the neighbouring state of Ch'î. Thither Confucius followed him, and there he would have remained, if he could have done so with advantage to the ruler of Ch'î and his government without compromising his own character. Finding it impossible to do so, he returned to Lû.

To the end of his brief period of office in B.C. 495.

26. After this, he continued without official employment for the long period of fourteen years. The expelled marquis having died in Ch'î, the rightful heir was set aside, and another member of the ruling House appointed in his place. The disorder of the state increased, and the wisdom of Confucius appeared in the prudence with which he steered his course, so as not to become the partizan of any of the ambitious chiefs.

Some say that during this period he divorced his wife, but the notion that he did do so has proceeded from an erroneous interpretation of a passage in the " Record of Rites." [1]

At length, in B.C. 500, when Confucius was

[1] See Note D.

fifty-one years old, some degree of order was restored, and he became chief magistrate of the town of Chung-tû, and a marvellous reformation of the manners of the people speedily took place. The marquis, astonished at what he saw, asked him whether a whole state could be governed by his rules, and was assured that they might be applied to the whole kingdom. Forthwith Confucius was made assistant-superintendent of Works, in which capacity he made many improvements in agriculture. The office of minister of Crime followed, and the appointment was enough to make an end of crime. There was no necessity to put the penal laws in execution. No offenders showed themselves.

For three years Confucius held this important office. The resistance to the supreme authority which had so much disturbed the state was possible through the fortified cities held by the great clans, which served the same purpose as the castles owned by the barons of Europe in the feudal ages. Confucius succeeded in dismantling several of these. " He strengthened," we are told, "the ruling House, and weakened the ministers and chiefs. A transforming government went abroad. Dishonesty and dissoluteness were ashamed, and hid their heads. Loyalty and good faith became the characteristics of the men, and chastity and docility .those of the women. Strangers came in crowds from other states." Confucius was the idol of the people, and flew in songs through their mouths.

But this success did not long gladden the heart of our hero. As the fame of his reformations went abroad, the neighbouring states began to be afraid. The marquis of Ch'î said, "With Confucius at the head of its government, Lû will become supreme among the states; and Ch'î, which is nearest to it, will be the first swallowed up. Let us propitiate it by a surrender of territory." One of his ministers suggested, however, that they should first try to separate between the marquis of Lû and his wise adviser. Beautiful women and fine horses were sent to Lû as baits, and by them the prince was taken. Confucius and his lessons were neglected. He felt that he could not retain office, that he ought not to remain in the state. "It is time for you to leave," said Tsze-lû to him. Most unwillingly and slowly, by short stages, he went away. He would have welcomed a message of recall. But none came.

Till his return to Lû in B.C. 483.

27. The sage was now in his fifty-sixth year, when he felt driven to forsake his native Lû ; and for thirteen years he travelled ˙ from one

feudal state to another, seeking rest and finding none, always hoping to meet with a ruler who would adopt his counsels, and always disappointed. Time would fail us if we were to follow him and his attendant disciples in all their wanderings. His fame had gone before him, and most of the princes whom he visited received him with distinction, and would gladly have given him office and retained him at their courts; but no one was prepared to accept his principles and act them out. Repeatedly, in travelling through the country, he and his companions were in straits, and even in peril of their lives. Once they were assailed by a mob, who mistook the master for an officer at whose hands they had suffered much. While the others were alarmed, he calmly said, "After the death of king Wăn, was not the cause of letters and truth lodged in me? If Heaven had wished to let this cause perish, I should not have got such a relation to it. While Heaven does not let the cause of truth perish, what can the men of K'wang do to me?" In the same way, on another occasion, when they were attacked by a band employed by a malicious officer called Hwan T'ui, Confucius observed, "Heaven has produced the virtue that is in me; what can Hwan T'ui do to me?"

I will mention only two additional incidents of this period. At one time the whole party was reduced to great distress by the failure of their provisions, and even Tsze-lû said to the master, " Has the superior man indeed to endure in this way ? " The reply was, " The superior man may indeed have to endure want ; but the mean man, in distress, gives way to unbridled license." The distress, it is said, continued seven days, during which time Confucius maintained his equanimity, and was even cheerful, playing on his lute and singing. He retrained, however a deep impression of the perils of the occasion, and recurred to them in after years, recalling the men who had then been his faithful companions.

The other incident is of a different character, and shows us the sage in one of his lighter moods. One of the princelets through whose territory they passed, and who had never seen him, asked Tsze-lû how he would describe him. The disciple did not venture a reply ; but when Confucius heard of the circumstance, he said to him, " Why did you not say that I am simply a man who in his eager pursuit of knowledge forgets his food, who in the joy of its attainment forgets his sorrows, and who does not perceive that old age is coming on ? "

From his return to his death, B.C. 483—478.

28. It was brought about, how I need not detail, that he returned at length to Lû in B.C. 483. The marquis and his ministers received him respectfully, but he can hardly be said to have re-entered public life. Only five more years remained to him, and he devoted them mainly to the literary pursuits which had long occupied him. He had in hand also the compilation of the annals of Lû that we still possess under the name of the "Spring and Autumn." The year 482 was marked by the death of his son Lî, which did not affect him so much as that of his favourite Yen Hui, in the next year. Then he cried out, "Alas! Heaven is destroying me! Heaven is destroying me!" The other disciples had to admonish him of the excessive character of his grief. And in 479, Tsze-lû, perhaps the best loved after Yen Hui, met with a violent end. The master had foreboded that he would do so; but when the event came, he wept sore. And his own death was not far off. It took place in the spring of the following year, B.C. 478.

Early one morning, we are told, he got up; and, with his hands behind his back, dragging his staff, he moved about by the door, crooning over,

> " The great mountain must crumble ;
> The strong beam must break ;
> And the wise man wither away like a plant."

After a little he entered the house, and sat down opposite the door. Tsze-kung had heard his words, and said to himself, " If the great mountain crumble, to what shall I look up ? If the strong beam break, and the wise man wither away, on whom shall I lean ? I fear the master is going to be ill." With this he hastened into the house, when Confucius told him a dream which he had had in the night, and which he thought presaged his death, adding, " No intelligent monarch arises ; there is no prince in the kingdom who will make me his master. My time has come to die." So it was. He took to his couch, and after seven days expired.

Such is the account we have of the last days of the great philosopher of China. His end was not unimpressive, but it was melancholy. He uttered no prayer, and he betrayed no apprehension. " The mountain falling came to nought, and the rock was removed out of his place. So death prevailed against him, and he passed ; his countenance was changed, and he was sent away."

His disciples buried him with extraordinary pomp, and many of them built huts, and remained mourning near his grave as for a father for three years; and when the others were gone, the faithful Tsze-kung continued his reverent and affectionate vigil for another period of the same duration. Seven years ago I made a pilgrimage to the tomb of the master outside the city of Chü-fâu in Shan-tung. Musing on many things, I walked round and round, and ascended, the large mound of which the dust of Confucius must now form a part, and where bushes of the plant that supplies the divining stalks were growing. I also stood by the little house which is supposed to enclose the ground where Tsze-kung built his hut.

Memorabilia of Confucius.—His personal characteristics.

In the "Confucian Analects," a compilation that must have been formed by the disciples, and in portions of "The Record of Rites," we have abundant information of the sayings and doings of the sage. A whole book of the Analects is occupied with his personal characteristics;—his deportment, his eating, and his dress. It shows him to us at court, in his own house, in his carriage, in his bed. He was nice in his diet, but he was not a great eater. He laid down no precise limit to himself in the use of wine, or whatever drink was then used at meals in China ; but he did not allow himself to be confused by it. Although the food might be coarse rice and poor soup, he would, with a grave respectful air, offer a little of it in sacrifice; but it is not said to whom the offering was made.[1] On occasion of sudden thunder or violent wind he would change countenance; and also when he saw a person in mourning. When any of his friends died, if there were no relatives who could be depended on for the necessary offices, he would say, " I will bury him."

From the multitude of these memoranda we get a very complete idea of the man. At one time, when I compared them with the different style of our gospels, I was offended by them. I have long learned, however, to welcome them. They are the tribute to Confucius of admiration and love from those among whom he had for many years gone in and out.

[1] This was a practice something like our saying grace. The offering was made, according to the commentators, to the worthy or worthies who first taught the art of cooking. An analogous practice is referred to in two lines of an ancient poem (Shih, II. v., Ode 2) :

" With a handful of grain I go out and divine,
How I may be able to become good."

Confucius did not change or modify the ancient religion.

29. But have we reason to think, as some have done,[1] that he made any changes in the ancient religion of China, or modified its records at all, when they passed through his hands? I must answer this question in the negative. I have shown in different works that his labours on the ancient classics were not so extensive as has been generally supposed. He studied them, and exhorted and helped his disciples to do the same, but he did not alter them, nor even digest them into their present form.

His enunciating the golden rule.

30. His greatest achievement in the inculcation of morality was his formulating the golden rule, which is not found in its condensed expression in the old classics. The merit of it is his own. We find it repeatedly in the Analects, the Doctrine of the Mean, and the Great Learning. Tsze-kung once asked him if there were one word which would serve as a rule of conduct for all the life; and he replied, "Is not reciprocity such a word?—What you do not want done to

[1] Hardwick's "Christ and other Masters," Pt. III., pp. 18, 19.

yourself, do not do to others." Subsequently, when the disciple told him that he was carrying this rule into practice, he replied, " Ts'ze, you have not attained to that." He was thus aware of the difficulty of obeying the precept, and he confessed on one occasion that he himself failed to do so. His words then also showed that the rule had for him not only a negative form, but also a positive form. He was unable, he said, to take the initiative in serving his father as he would require his son to serve him ; and so of the other relations between ruler and minister, elder brother and younger, friend and friend.[1] Chinese critics contend that in so speaking Confucius was only using the language of humility ; but evidently he was speaking the truth, and we do not think the worse of him when we find that, like other men, he was compassed with infirmity.

So far, therefore, as the morality of the religion of China was concerned, the sage invigorated it by this golden maxim. If it be said that he arrived at it from his analysis of human nature, and laid it down without a divine sanction, it must be remembered that with him, as with T'ang and others of the great ancients, man's nature was the distinguishing endowment given

[1] "Doctrine of the Mean," ch. 13.

to him by Heaven, or God, and that the path which it indicated was the will of God concerning his duty. There could be no testimony on this point more express than what we have in the first sentence of the Doctrine of the Mean : —"What Heaven has conferred is called the nature; an accordance with this nature is called the path of duty; the regulation of this path is called instruction."

What is to be thought of him as a religious teacher.

31. But it is not in the sphere of morality so much as in that of religion that fault is found with Confucius. I have complained myself of his avoiding the personal name of Tî, or God, and only using the more indefinite term Heaven. Only one case occurs to me in which he used the personal and relative name excepting when he was quoting from the old books; that case being his vindication, as related in the former Lecture, of the solstitial services, whether performed at the altar of heaven or that of earth, as being equally rendered to God. His avoiding the name Tî seems to betray a coldness of temperament and intellect in the matter of religion; and yet when we consider how the public worship of God was restricted to the

sovereign as the representative of the people,
it may have been that Confucius felt himself
fettered, and did not care to use the personal
name. He need not have been so; but that
" Heaven " was to him the name of a personal
being appears not only from the instances of
his employment of it already adduced, but from
these two others : " He who offends against
Heaven has none to whom he can pray ; " and
again, " Alas ! there is no one that knows me ! "
to which he immediately subjoined, " But there
is Heaven ;—It knows me ! "

It has been said, again, that the definition of
wisdom which he gave to the disciple Fan Ch'ih
was likely to make him doubt the existence of
spiritual beings, or at least to make him slight
their worship. " To give one's self," said he,
" to the duties due to men, and while respecting
spiritual beings, to keep aloof from them, may
be called wisdom." But we had occasion to
approve the warning which he gave against
sacrificing to spirits with whom we have no
legitimate connexion.[1] It might turn out, if we
knew all about Fan Ch'ih, that what the master
said to him was to the same effect as that warning. And indeed the worship of ancestors and
of the departed great was a practice of such

[1] Page 92.

doubtful propriety, and so liable to abuse, that I am pleased to think that Confucius wished to guard his disciples and others against the superstition and other evils to which it might lead. No one could be more observant of it when he believed it to be right, than he was. " He sacrificed (to the dead)," it is said, "as if they were present; he sacrificed to the spirits, as if the spirits were present."

This charge against Confucius, then, must be dismissed as not proven. Nor was he a mere formalist, clinging to the dead letter of an institution when the spirit had all gone out of it. Generally, no moral teacher ever required more stringently an inward sincerity than he did; and the power of example—influence rather than force—has quite an important place in his teachings. But he was conservative in his tendencies, and wisdom existed to his view in the past. He did not understand how

"The old order changeth, yielding place to new,
And God fulfils himself in many ways,
Lest one good custom should corrupt the world."

My meaning will appear from the following instance. In the end of every year the feudal princes received from the Court of Châu a calendar for the next year, and each of them, on the first day of every month, should have

repaired to his ancestral temple, sacrificed a
sheep to the founder of his line, and requested
leave to go on to the duties of the new month.
But in Confucius' time the lords of Lû had long
ceased to do their part in this ceremony, though
the sheep was still sacrificed in the temple.
Tsze-kung in these circumstances wished to
abolish the custom altogether, but the master
said to him, "You grudge the loss of the sheep ;
I grudge the loss of the ceremony." That is,
while the form remained, he thought that the
spirit of it might be brought back. The dry
bones might live. In that hope Confucius was
in error, but the instance suffices to show that
his formalism was not for the form's sake.

Once more, it is said that he discountenanced
the use of prayer ; but the passage on which
this charge is based is insufficient to sustain it,
and contains, moreover, Confucius' own declaration that he did pray. On some occasion when
he was very ill,[1] Tsze-lû asked leave to pray for
him, and when the master hesitated, doubting
whether such a thing were proper, referred to
some book of prayers, and quoted from it to
the effect that prayer might be made to the

---

[1] Analects, VII., ch. 34.   I have seen a statement somewhere that this incident took place during Confucius' last
illness, but the death of Tsze-lû had taken place before
that.

spirits of heaven and earth. All that Confucius said in reply was, "My praying has been for a long time." We do not know what he meant. He may have wished to disabuse the disciple's mind of some superstitious notion on the subject of prayer. The utmost that can be surmised from it is that his piety was not demonstrative or effusive.

Two things that lower our estimate of him.

32. While thus defending Confucius from some charges that have been brought against him, I must not be silent about two things that lead us to think less highly of him than it may seem to you that I do. We have rejoiced in his enunciation of the golden rule ;—Lâo-tsze had advanced even beyond this in the field of morality, and said, "Return good for evil." Some one of Confucius' school heard the maxim, and, being puzzled by it, consulted the master. He also was puzzled, formed a syllogism in his mind about it, and replied, "What then will you return for good ? Recompense injury with justice, and return good for good." Well, justice is good, and I do not think that Confucius had any thought of vengeance when he used the term ; but if we only do good to them that do good

to us, what reward have we? I wish the sage
had risen to the height of the thought that was
put before him. The other thing is the execution of the historical work called "The Spring
and Autumn," which contains the annals of Lû
for two hundred and forty-two years, down to
within two years of Confucius' death. Mencius
regarded it as the greatest of the master's
achievements, and says that its appearance struck
terror into rebellious ministers and unfilial sons.
The author himself had a similar opinion of it,
and said that it was from it that men would know
him, and also (some of them) condemn him. Was
his own heart misgiving him, when he thus spake
of men condemning him for the Ch'un Ch'iû? The
fact is that the annals are astonishingly meagre,
and not only so, but evasive and deceptive.
' The Ch'un Ch'iû," says Kung-yang, who commented on it and supplemented it within a
century after its composition,—"the Ch'un Ch'iû
conceals (the truth) out of regard to the high
in rank, to kinship, and to men of worth." And
I have shown in the fifth volume of my Chinese
Classics, that this "concealing" covers all the
ground embraced in our three English words—
ignoring, concealing, and misrepresenting. What
shall we say to these things? It has been observed that "charges have been brought against

Confucius of want of truthfulness, but if we examine them, they dwindle down to the mere question of what is truth." [1] This consideration ought to silence certain charges that have been made from unimportant incidents in the sage's career, but it does not solve the difficulty in regard to him that arises from the style of the Ch'un Ch'iû. No answer can be given to the question—not a small one—What is truth ? that will meet the case of the historian who ignores, conceals, and misrepresents events he is writing about. I often wish that I could cut the knot by denying the genuineness and authenticity of the " Spring and Autumn " as we now have it; but the chain of evidence that binds it to the hand and pencil of Confucius in the close of his life is very strong. And if a foreign student take so violent a method to enable him to look at the character of the philosopher without this flaw of historical untruthfulness, the governors of China and the majority of its scholars will have no sympathy with him, and no compassion for his mental distress. Truthfulness was one of the subjects that Confucius often insisted on with his disciples; but the Ch'un Ch'iû has led his countrymen to conceal

[1] " Confucianism and Tâoism," (Society for Promoting Christian Knowledge,) p. 146.

the truth from themselves and others, wherever they think it would injuriously affect the reputation of the empire, or of its sages. But I hasten to bring the Lecture to a conclusion, and am very sorry to have, in the interest of truth, to leave Confucius under a cloud. I would only further remark that there is no valid authority for a saying often attributed to him that " in the west the true saint must be looked for and found."[1]

The admiration of Confucius among his disciples.

One of the most remarkable things is the impression that the sage made upon his disciples. Many of them were among the ablest men in China of their time, " superior men," mighty in word and deed ; and yet with them originated the practice of speaking of Confucius as " the greatest man that had ever lived," " far superior to Yâo and Shun," " like the Ch'î-lin among quadrupeds, the phœnix among birds, the T'âi mountain among mounds and ant-hills, and rivers and seas compared with rain-pools." He had gained their hearts and won their entire admiration. They began the pæan which has since resounded through all the intervening ages,

[1] See Note E.

nor is its swell less loud and confident now than it was nearly four-and-twenty centuries ago.

Estimate of Confucius by the government and people of China.

The "powers that be" in China joined ere long in the chorus of the disciples. Among Confucius' last words, we saw, were these,— "No intelligent monarch arises; there is no prince in the kingdom who will take me as his master." But he had hardly passed from the stage of life when the great ones of the nation began to acknowledge his merit, and to build temples and offer worship to him. Ch'in Shih Hwang Tî, the founder of the Ch'in dynasty in B.C. 221, found the name, and followers of Confucius his greatest obstacles when he wished, after overthrowing the feudal system, to make a new empire according to his own ideas. He wielded the sword and kindled the flame against them, but in vain. He might have said on his death-bed, in words analogous to those used by the Roman Julian, "Thou hast conquered, O Master K'ung."

In A.D. 1 there began the practice of conferring, by imperial authority, honorary titles on Confucius, and in the year 57 it was enacted that sacrifices should be offered to him in the government colleges throughout the country. At the present day he is worshipped twice a year on certain days in the middle months of spring and autumn. Then the emperor goes in state to the imperial college in Peking, and performs his homage, and presents the appointed offerings, before the spirit-tablets of Confucius, and four of his most famous disciples. These are the words of the principal prayer on the occasion :—" On this month of this year, I, the emperor, offer sacrifice to the philosopher K'ung, the ancient Teacher, the perfect Sage, and say, O Teacher, in virtue equal to heaven and earth, whose doctrines embrace the time past and the present, thou didst digest and transmit the six classics, and didst hand down lessons for all generations ! Now in this second month of spring (or autumn), in reverent observance of the old statutes, with victims, silks, spirits, and fruits, I offer sacrifice to thee. With thee are associated the philosopher Yen, continuator of thee ; the philosopher Tsăng, exhibitor of thy fundamental principles ; the philosopher Tsze-sze, transmitter of thee ; and the philosopher Măng, second to thee. Mayst thou enjoy the offerings !" So is the sage K'ung, who was unreasonably neglected when alive, now unreasonably worshipped when dead

The imperial prayer is the fullest vindication of my treating of the ancient religion of China under the name of Confucianism. K'ung was a great and wonderful man; but I think that the religion which he found, and did so much to transmit to posterity, was still greater and more remarkable than he.

NOTES ON LECTURE II.

NOTE A, p. 93.

While passing in the Lecture from the subject of sacrifice or religious worship in the Confucian religion, I subjoin the following condensed account of it as it existed in the Châu times, and as with some modifications it exists still, taken from the Record of Rites, 1., Part II. iii. 6, 7 :—

" The son of Heaven sacrificed to heaven and earth ; to (the rulers of) the four quarters, to the (spirits of all the) hills and rivers ; and offered the five (domestic) sacrifices ; —all in the course of the year.

" The feudal princes sacrificed to (the rulers of) their several quarters ; to the (spirits of their) hills and rivers ; and offered the five (domestic) sacrifices ;—all in the course of the year.

" Great officers offered the five (domestic) sacrifices,— all in the course of the year.

" (Other) officers sacrificed to their forefathers.

" There was no presuming to resume any sacrifice that had been discontinued (by proper authority), or to discontinue one which had been so established. A sacrifice which it is not proper to offer, and which yet is offered, is named a licentious sacrifice. A licentious sacrifice brings no blessing."

The student who has read the many pages of commentary on these sentences in the imperial edition of the

Lî, issued in the present dynasty, will have gained a sufficient acquaintance with the bones or skeleton of Chinese
worship, and the differences of native scholars on various
points. All agree in maintaining that the sacrifices to
forefathers were open to all, "from the son of Heaven
down to the common people."

NOTE B, p. 121.

In J. M. Callery's translation of an "Expurgated Record
of Rites," published in 1833, he gives for these sentences,
—"Tsâi-wo (disciple de Confucius) dit (à son maître),
'J'ai entendu souvent les noms d'Ame et d'Esprit, mais
j'ignore ce qu'ils signifient.' Confucius dit, ' La respiration
de l'homme est une manifestation de l'Esprit, le corps est
une manifestation de l'Ame. La réunion des mots Ame
et Esprit en une seule expression Kwei-Shăn (Ame-Esprit)
est un sujet d'enseignement sublime.' "
What follows is not translated, as being expunged from
his text. On the above he has the following note :—
"Confucius semble distinguer dans l'homme deux substances immatérielles ayant avec le corps des rapports
différents, distinction qui rappelle les subtilités à peine
spirituelles de Jh. de Maistre sur l'esprit vital. Mais chez
le philosophe Chinois les théories psychologiques ont peu
d'importance ; il ne les regarde que comme les bonnes à
intimider ou à encourager le vulgaire ignorant, et ne les
traite, par conséquent que d'une manière toute super-
ficielle, s'arrêtant plutôt aux mots qu'aux idées. C'est un
des faits les plus remarquables dans l'histoire de l'esprit
humain, que les Chinois n'aient jamais tenté sérieusement
d'approfonder les mystères de l'âme."
I have no doubt that Confucius told his disciple all that
he himself knew of the subject they were talking about.
Whatever "the mysteries of the soul" may be, Confucius
must have come to the conclusion that they were beyond
his ken and research.

NOTE C, p. 124.

Dr. Morrison, in his Dictionary, I. i., page 710, says that
" Confucius was a bastard son of Shù Liang-ho, and a
daughter of the Yen family, who cohabited in the
wilderness." His authority for this statement is the
seventeenth of Sze-ma Ch'ien's Histories and Biographies ;
but Ch'ien's language is translated with needless harshness.
All that it may mean is that there was some irregularity
in the union of the parties. Chiang Yung (1761) thinks
that the disparity of their age is sufficient to satisfy Ch'ien's
text. A gloss in the " Record of Rites," under II. i. *1*,
par. 10, suggests that the phrase refers to some incomplete-
ness or informality in the arrangements for the marriage.
All that we can say is that the statement is disrespectful to
Confucius. Considering the Tâoist proclivities of Ch'ien,
I think it was only a gibe on the age of Shû Liang-ho.

Latterly, it has become the practice of some writers to
say that " Confucius himself was born of a concubine"
(Report of the Committee on C. D. Act ; Hong-kong,
1879)." But I do not know of any authority for such
a statement. The account in the " Narratives of the
School" says that Shû Liang-ho, having nine daughters,
and no son, by his wife, and only a son who was a cripple
by his concubine, sought for another marriage, and applied
to a gentleman of the Yen family, who gave him his
youngest daughter to wife (Chiâ Yü, IX., art. 2). In order
to marry the new wife, Liang-ho must have divorced the
old one, and the fact of her having no son was a sufficient
reason, according to the law of China, for his doing so.
That he actually did so is implied in the paragraph of
the " Record of Rites " which is discussed in the next note.

The care which Confucius took to bury his mother in
the same grave with his father also implies that they
were husband and wife. The sage was neither a bastard,
nor the son of a concubine. He might have been either

without any disgrace to himself, but an impartial student of history will not readily give ear to reports that will by many be considered discreditable to his subject.

NOTE D, p. 128.

In the " Record of Rites," II. i. par. 4, we have the following incident of life in the Confucian family :— " When the mother of Tsze-shang "—great-grandson of Confucius—" died, and he did not perform any of the mourning rites for her, the disciples of his father Tsze-sze asked whether the former superior man had not performed those rites for his divorced mother. Tsze-sze having replied that he had, they asked him why he did not make his son do so for his mother. ' My predecessor, the superior man,' said he, ' failed in no proper course. When it was proper to behave generously, he did so ; when it was proper to restrain his generosity, he restrained it. But I cannot attain to this. When she was my wife, she was my son's mother ; when she was not my wife, she ceased to be his mother.' In this way the custom of the K'ung family not to mourn for a divorced mother originated with Tsze-sze."

Who is meant by " the former superior man " in this passage? Does it mean Tsze-sze's father? or his grand-father? If the former, then Confucius had divorced his wife ; if the latter, then Shû Liang-ho had divorced his, as I have contended in the preceding note that he did, and the mother of Confucius was not a concubine ; but though a second, yet a proper wife. That " the former superior man," who always pursued the proper course, is more likely to be Confucius than his son Lî, may be considered as self-evident.

The twenty-eighth paragragh of the same book also bears on the point in hand. It says : " When the mother of Po-yü "—Confucius' son, Lî—" died, he continued to wail for her after the twelve months "—proper for such a demonstration of grief—"were ended." The master heard the noise, and asked who it was that was thus wailing. Being told by the disciples that it was Lî, he said, "Pshaw! it's too much;" and when Po-yü was told of the remark, he ceased to wail."

The attempts to explain this passage in harmony with the assumption that Confucius divorced his wife are unnatural. The editors of the imperial edition of the Lî Chî say upon it that there is nowhere any mention of such a thing, and that the old view on the subject seems to be a mistake. As Confucius' wife did not die till B.C. 485, when he was sixty-six, and had thus been his partner for nearly fifty years, we do think that he might have had more sympathy with the wailing of his son for her. He could show signs of excessive sorrow himself at times, as when his favourite disciple Yen Hui died ;—the "Pshaw! it's too much," does not make us admire him. Still there is really no evidence that he divorced his wife.

NOTE E, p. 146.

In "The Ten Great Religions," by James Freeman Clarke (Boston, U.S., 1871), page 58, the author says :—"Confucius is a star in the east, to lead his people to Christ. One of the most authentic of his sayings is this, that 'in the west the true saint must be looked for and found.' He had a perception, such as truly great men have often had, of some one higher than himself who was to come after him." The only saying having any likeness to this and attributed to Confucius is in the works of the philosopher Lieh, a Tâoist writer not long posterior to our sage. His fourth book has the name of "Chung-nî" after Confucius (that being his cognomen) ; and it is related in it that a great officer of Ch'ăn, having come on a mission to Lû, was told at a private interview with the Head of the Shû-sun family that there was a sage in the state. The visitor asked, "Do you not mean K'ung Ch'iû (Confucius)?" Being answered in the affirmative, he asked "How do you know that K'ung is sage?" The chief replied, "I have heard from Yen Hui that K'ung Ch'iû can dispense with his mind, and use (only) his body." The visitor said, "In my state also there is a sage. Do you not know it?" and went on to say that this sage was a Kăng Ts'ang, a disciple of Lâo Tan, whose tâo he had mastered, so that he could see with his ears and hear with his eyes. This being reported to the marquis of Lû, he was greatly excited, and sent to Ch'ăn and invited Kăng Ts'ang to come to him. Mr. Kăng accordingly came to Lû, and, when received and questioned about what had been reported of him, said that the report was incorrect ; that he could see and hear without using either his eyes or ears, but that one sense could not be made to discharge the function of another. He then attempted to explain how he had acquired so wonderful a gift. The marquis was delighted, and by-and-by related the whole conversation to Confucius, who, it is said, smiled, and gave him no reply.

Apparently without any connexion with the above story there follows an account of an interview between a high minister of the state of Sung and Confucius. The former said to the other, "Are you a sage?" "How should I presume to count myself a sage?" was the reply ; "but I am extensively learned, and have a memory richly stored." The minister then asked if the three kings, the founders of the dynasties of Châu, Shang, and Hsiâ, had been sages ; and Confucius allowed them the merit of wisdom and valour, yet said he did not know that they were sages. The cases of the five Tí and three Hwang, stretching back into the prehistoric time, were similarly disposed of, till the visitor was struck aghast, and asked, "Who then can be considered a sage?" Confucius looked moved for a time, and said, "Among the people of the western regions there is a sage. Without exercising any government, he secures that there is no disorder ; without his speaking, faith is reposed in him as a matter of course ; without his transforming, transformation naturally goes on. How vast (his merit) ! The people can find no name for it. But I doubt whether (even) he be a sage ; I do not know whether he is truly a sage, or truly not a sage." The minister of Sung silently reflected in his heart, and said to himself, " K'ung Ch'iû is mocking me."

This is the whole of the passage, from which is derived the "most authentic saying" of Confucius quoted by Mr. Clarke. And inquiries have come to me from France and Germany asking me for information about "the un- conscious prophecy" of the Chinese sage. The whole story is from a Tâoist mint, and intended to exalt the tâo in the first place. We may safely conclude that Con- fucius never said anything of the kind. In the sentence beginning, "Among the people of the western regions," and the next one, the verbs may be translated in the present tense or the past :—" There is a sage," or "there was a sage," etc., but they cannot be construed in the future. Among the notes in the "General Mirror of History," appended to the eighth year of the emperor Ming of the Han dynasty, there is one to the effect that "the name of the sage of the west mentioned in Lieh-tsze is Budh." The Buddhists have as much right to claim "the unconscious prophecy" for Buddha as Christians have for Christ; that is, neither have any right to claim it.

III.

TAOISM:
AS A RELIGION AND A PHILOSOPHY.

"Intruding into those things which he hath not seen."—
Colossians ii. 18.

道 於 幾 水 若 善 上

"The highest goodness is like water, the nature of which is near to Tâo."—*The Tâo Teh King*, ch. 8.

"Whosoever exalteth himself shall be abased, and he that humbleth himself shall be exalted."—*Luke* xiv. 11.

III.

What is Tâoism ?

1. I HAVE often been asked what Tâoism is, and I have no doubt the question is now in many of your minds, and you are hoping to receive an answer to it from my lecture. But the question is a difficult one, and I will not anticipate myself by attempting a definition of the name at the outset. It has two different applications ;—first, to a popular and widely-spread religion of China ; and then to the system of thought in the remarkable treatise called the Tâo Teh King, written in the sixth century B.C. by Lâo-tsze. In other words, Tâoism is the name both of a religion and a philosophy. The author of the philosophy is the chief god, or one at least of the chief gods, of the religion ; but there is no evidence that the religion grew out of his book. It was impossible, indeed, as you will see, for it to do so in many of its aspects. Any relation between the two things is merely external, for in spirit

and tendency they are antagonistic. I will do my best to describe them both, so far as the time will allow, and you may be able to fashion for yourselves a definition of Tâoism in both the applications of the name, if after all I shall not be able to give it to you in categorical terms.

Before it became the practice to transfer to other languages the Chinese word Tâo, Tâoism was ordinarily called Rationalism,—a name admirably calculated to lead the mind astray as to what the religion is. And in the book, "Reason," as Dr. Chalmers says, "would be more like a quality or attribute of some conscious being than Tâo is."[1] You will understand from this that Tâo is not the name of a person, but of a concept or idea. Tâoism does not owe its name to its author, as Buddhism or Mohammedanism does. I will now endeavour to set forth, first, the religion, and next, the philosophy.

Legal standing of Tâoism in China.

2. Confucianism (as described in my two former lectures) is the religion *par excellence* of China ; but both Tâoism and Buddhism have a legal standing in the country. Their suppression

[1] The Speculations of "the Old Philosopher" (Lâo-tsze). Introduction, p. xi.   (Trübner & Co.)

has been recommended to the government at different times, and individual emperors have felt inclined to attempt it.[1] We saw how the Manchû emperor of the K'ang-hsî period prepared an edict against binding the feet of girls which he never ventured to issue.[2] In the same way he wished to undertake the suppression of Tâoism, but saw reason to abandon the project. Tâoism is among " the strange principles " or systems which the seventh precept of his sacred edict commands to be "discountenanced and banished," and it is derided in the public expositions of that edict; but nevertheless, and wisely, it is tolerated.

Tâoism officially recognised and its Chief endowed.

And it is also officially recognised and endowed. The late Mr. Mayers in his "Manual of the Chinese Government"[3] says:—"The Chinese official system, which allows no condition of the body politic to remain, in theory at least, unprovided with means for its control, includes

[1] See note A.

[2] P. 112.

[3] " The Chinese Government. A Manual of Chinese Titles, with an appendix." By William Frederick Mayers. P. 77. (Trübner & Co.) See note B.

among its administrative rules a complete system of ecclesiastical gradations of rank and authority in connexion with the priesthood of both the Buddhist religion and the Tâoist order. While refraining from interference with the internal organisation of either of those bodies, or with the admission of members to their ranks, the imperial Institutes provide a framework in harmony with the all-pervading official system, to be grafted on the hierarchy as it is found in either case developed according to its own traditional rules." I have no occasion to speak of the framework for Tâoism provided by the Government, further than that it centres in the pope or hereditary chief of the religion, whose seat is on the Lung-hû (Dragon-tiger) mountain, in the department of Kwang-hsin, Chiang-hsî. His surname is Chang, and he has the title of " Heavenly Master." The headship of Tâoism has been in the Chang family, with the exception of one period of interruption, since the first century of our era. The spirit of the first pope is supposed to have transmigrated from one chief to another down to the present time. Since A.D. 1015 the chiefs have possessed large tracts of land about the Lung-hû mountain, which were granted in that year as a perpetual endowment for the family to Chang

Chăng-sui by the emperor Chăn-tsung of the Sung dynasty.[1] One of the common sayings which I learned in China nearly forty years ago was this :—" However the empire be disordered and convulsed, the Changs and the K'ungs have no occasion to be troubled." I understood that the K'ungs were the descendants of Confucius, whose representative has always the title of "duke," and is endowed with extensive estates ; but it was a considerable time before I ascertained that the Changs were the popes of Tâoism.[2] There are other ways in which the existence and importance of Tâoism are recognized by the Government, and I hope to find opportunity to speak at least of one of them as I proceed with the subject. What I have now said sufficiently shows that the religion, though heterodox, has a legal standing in the country.

Origin of Tâoism as a religion. Its polytheism.

3. We traced Confucianism and its double worship of God and of ancestors back into pre-

---

[1] "The General Mirror of History" (T'ung chien Kang Mû), *in an.*

[2] See note C.

historic time ; but Tâoism as a religion did not exist until a considerable time after the commencement of our Christian era. There is not a word in the Tâo Têh King, of the sixth century B.C., that savours either of superstition or religion. In the works of Lieh-tsze and Chwang-tsze, followers of Lâo-tsze, two or three centuries later, we find abundance of grotesque superstition, though we are never sure how far those writers are sincere and really believed the things they relate; but their beliefs, if we can say that they had beliefs, had not become embodied in any religious institutions. When we come to the founder of the Ch'in dynasty, bestriding the Chinese world like a colossus, and waging fierce war against the memory and followers of Confucius, we become aware of the powerful hold that Tâoist superstition must have obtained in the country. He, the subjugator of the feudal states, extending his dominion over all the provinces that constitute the present China, building the great wall, and laying the foundations of the despotic rule that has continued to the present day,—he fits out expeditions and sends them to sea in quest of Făng-lâi and the other isles of the Immortals, and to bring to him from them the herb of immortality. The records of his brief reign do not tell us

whether he fully observed the state-worship that had been paid to God by all the preceding sovereigns of the kingdom ; but we know that he offered sacrifices to eight spirits, or eight lords as he called them, unknown before or since in the sacrificial canons.[1] If Shih Hwang-Tî had lived much longer, Tâoism would have developed into a religion quite different from what it has been and is.

When the dynasty of Ch'in passed away, soon after the beginning of the third century B.C., and that of Han took its place, Confucianism regained its pre-eminence. The superstitions, indeed, of Tâoism had become widely diffused. The emperor Wû, during the greater part of his long reign of fifty-six years, from B.C. 140 to 85, was a slave to them ; the Tâoist prejudices of the historian Sze-mâ Ch'ien, whose great work appeared about B.C. 100, are universally acknowledged. The second and third emperors of the eastern Han dynasty invited Chang Tâo-ling, the first of the popes or patriarchs of Tâoism, to come to court. Not-

---

[1] See Mayers' Chinese Reader's Manual, pp. 337, 338. It is remarkable that Shih Hwang-Tî's first God was called by him T'ien Chû, " Lord of Heaven," the very name for God now used, by papal authority and command, by the Roman Catholic missionaries.

withstanding these things, Confucianism was
still the sole religion of China ; but in the year
A.D. 65 Buddhism was introduced from India.
Its missionaries, bringing with them an image of
Buddha, were received with distinction at court ;
a building was assigned to them for a temple
and monastery ; Buddhism ere long made itself
felt in many parts of the country. Buddhists
and Tâoists were from the first drawn together
by various affinities. But the latter also saw
that if they would retain their influence with
the people, they must have temples and monas-
teries and public services like the former. It
has not yet been clearly ascertained when they
began to erect these buildings. The main body
of the literature of China is Confucian, and the
research necessary to obtain information on
subjects lying outside of it is great ; but
information on the point in hand will be
forthcoming when the desirableness of it has
been recognized. Of the great and all but
overmastering influence of Buddhism on the
development of Tâoism there is no doubt,
and I will content myself here with one illustration of it. You go into a Buddhist temple
in China, and what strikes you most at first
sight is the three gigantic images in the principal hall, called the San Pâo or "Three Precious

Ones."[1] You know that in the theory of Buddhism "the three precious ones" are Intelligence personified in Buddha, the Law, and the Church; but an attendant of the temple will tell you that the images represent Buddha past, present, and to come. The common people, ignorant of the esoteric view of a Trinity, cannot understand the logical abstractions that are thus represented, and blindly worship what they suppose are three divinities; and when you stand, as I have often done, a long time before the great figures, you feel that you are sympathizing with their popular worshippers more than with the philosophers.

You go now into a Tâoist temple, and are immediately confronted by three vast images, which you mistake at first for the precious Buddhas. By-and-by you see that they are different, and understand that they are San Chʻing, "the three Pure or Holy Ones": "the Perfect Holy One;" "the Highest Holy One;" and "the Greatest Holy One." Each of them has the title of Tʻien Tsun, "the Heavenly and Honoured," and also the title of Shang Tî or God, the latter taken from the Confucian or old religion of the country. The second of the three is "the Most High Prince Lâo," the usual

[1] See Eitel's Handbook of Chinese Buddhism, p. 150, Article Triratna.

style in speaking of Lâo-tsze; but his full title is "the greatest Holy One, (the Lord) of Tâo and Virtue, the Heavenly and Honoured." The first of the three, "the Perfect (literally, Gemmeous) Holy One, who was at the first beginning, the Heavenly and Honoured," is also called "P'an-kû, or Chaos."[1] P'an-kû is spoken of by the common people as "the first man, who opened up heaven and earth."   It has been said to me in "pidgin" English that "he is all the same your Adam;" and in Tâoist picture-books I have seen him as a shaggy, dwarfish, Hercules, developing from a bear rather than an ape, and wielding an immense hammer and chisel with which he is breaking the chaotic rocks. You may think that I am caricaturing the representations in this highest department of Tâoism, but I am not conscious of doing so. The utmost that I can discern in them is the crude notion of a gross mind that the present visible universe,—"the heavens and the earth and all the host of them,"—was fashioned somehow out of a previously existing chaos.   But when Tâoism ranks Chaos, "anarch old," as one of

[1] Morrison's Dictionary, I. i., p. 15; "View of China for Philological Purposes," p. 111; and Chalmers' "Collection of Tâoist Words and Phrases," in Doolittle's Vocabulary and Handbook, II., p. 235.

its Trinity of great Gods, we are prepared to find what is fantastic and unreasonable in its system. Is Chaos any better than Chance, "that unspiritual God and miscreator"? The "three Holy Ones" are styled "Gods of void non-existence." Next to them is Yü Hwang Shang Tî, the "gemmeous sovereign, God," who has in a great measure displaced the others from the public mind, superintending, as he is supposed to do, all human affairs, and also exercising a control over the physical world. He is styled " the God of mysterious existence." The Tâoists contend that he is the same with the Shang Tî of the classics, forgetting that that Shang Tî was worshipped by the sage Shûn, more than two thousand years before Tâoism had assumed the form of a religion. And more than this. The original of this popular idol was a magician of the Chang family that has given so many patriarchs to Tâoism, whose deification cannot be traced higher than the T'ang dynasty, in our seventh or eighth century. The most extravagant legends are written about him. He and another magician called Liû, rode a race on dragons up to heaven, which was won by Chang.[1]

[1] Essay by Dr. Edkins, read at the Missionary Conference, Shanghâi, in 1877.

Tâoism has many more "gods," "supreme gods," "celestial gods," "great gods," and "divine rulers." The name Tî, or God, which Confucianism never abused and prostituted to such an extent, never indeed abused at all without calling forth some protest and in the end correction of the error, is given to scores of the Tâoist deities. No polytheism could be more pronounced, or more grotesque, with hardly a single feature of poetic fancy or æsthetical beauty.

What Tâoism was before Buddhism came into China,—a mass of superstitions and sacrifices not digested into any system. Illustrated by the case of the Han emperor Wû.

4. It is evident that the influence of Buddhism did much to mould the form that Tâoism as a religion took. To understand the subject fully we must get some idea of what it was as a superstition or congeries of superstitions before it came into contact with the system from India; and that you may do this I will translate an account that we possess of the emperor Wû, of the Han dynasty, whom I have already mentioned. Having succeeded to the throne at an early age in B.C. 140, he was admonished by a distinguished

scholar to hold fast to Confucianism, and avoid prevalent superstitions.[1]   But the warning proved of no avail.   "The young sovereign," it is said, was naturally addicted to reverence and worship spiritual beings ; and when Lî Shâo-chün discoursed to him about the sacrifice to (the spirit of) the furnace and the art of keeping back the approach of age, he per-formed the sacrifice himself, and sent magicians to sea to search for the isle of Făng-lâi.   At the same time he engaged in alchemical studies, and attempted to transform cinnabar and other substances into gold.   After a long time Shâo-chün fell ill and died, but the emperor would not believe that he was really dead.   He said that he had simply been transformed and gone away as an Immortal, and employed men to carry on the exercise of his arts.

"The year after, Shâo-wăng, a man of Ch'î, represented that he was possessed of wonderful arts, and was favourably received.   Just at that time a favourite inmate of the harem died, and Shâo-wăng contrived to make a spirit, in form resembling the deceased, appear to the emperor at night, who was so pleased that he gave the magician the rank of General with the title of "the accomplished and complete," and treated

[1] See note A.

him as an honoured guest. Before two years, however, his arts had become feeble, on which he got an ox to swallow a piece of silk with a writing on it prepared by himself, and told the emperor that it had been made known to him that the animal had a wonderful document in its belly. The ox was killed, and the silk found, but the emperor recognized the handwriting, and "the accomplished and complete" was put to death.

"Not daunted by the death of this charlatan, a former fellow-student of his, called Lwan Tâ, boasted to the emperor about his science, and affirmed that his master had said,—That other metals might be transmuted into gold; that the medicine of immortality might be obtained; and that the Immortals might be made to appear. The emperor raised him also to the rank of General, and gave him a noble lady in marriage, so that the empire rang with the good fortune of the adventurer; but having spoken incautiously of seeing his master, and his arts all proving unsuccessful, he also was put to death.

"In the winter of that same year there was a Kung-sun Ch'ing, who was looking out for spirits in Ho-nan, and reported that he had seen the footprint of an Immortal on the wall

of Hâu-shih. On this the emperor repaired
to the east, and along the sea-coast offered
sacrifices to the eight spirits which Shih Hwang-
Tî had formerly worshipped. He also prepared
many vessels, and, filling them with several
thousand men who said that in the ocean
there were isles peopled by spirits, sent them
to find Făng-lâi and its inhabitants. He himself meanwhile returned to Făng Kâo; and
while there he raised a tumulus on mount T'âi.
At that time there was neither wind nor rain,
and the magicians said that it was just the
season to get hold of the spiritual beings
of Făng-lâi. Joyfully the emperor turned
his face again to the east, full of hope to
have his wishes fulfilled every hour, and from
the shore looked out for his longed-for visitors;
but it was all in vain.

"Five years after, he again went and sacrificed
on mount Tâi, and in the course of twelve years
had gone all round to the five great mountains
and four great rivers, sacrificing; but of all that
the magicians promised from their looking out
for spirits and seeking on the sea for the isle
of Făng-lâi, not a single thing came to pass.

"In the year B.C. 99, the emperor, after
ploughing the imperial field at Chü-lû, repaired
to mount T'âi, and performed the usual services

there, saying at the close of them, to his atten-
dants, "Since I ascended the throne, by wild
and unreasonable practices I have greatly
distressed the empire. I regret the past, but
cannot repair its errors. Henceforth, however,
I will do away with everything that is injurious
to the common people, and wastes the resources
of the country. T'ien Ch'ien-ch'iû, chief of the
court of ceremonies, said, "The stories of the
magicians about spirits and Immortals are
very numerous, but not one of them has been
made good. Your majesty should make an
end of them." "T'ien's words are good," said
the emperor. His commands were issued
accordingly, but ever afterwards he would
often say to his ministers with sorrow, "Alas
that I was so led astray by the magicians!
Are there anywhere such Immortal beings as
they speak of? Their talk is all extravagance
and folly. If we are temperate in our diet,
and use medicine, we may make our illnesses
few. That is all we can attain to."[1]

The above is a condensed account of the
Tâoist practices of the emperor Wû. It might
have been very much enlarged, and I am sorry

[1] Liang Yen-nien's Illustrated edition of the K'ang-hsi
Sacred Edict, with a little addition from the "General
Mirror of History."

it does not mention the astrological superstitions to which he gave heed. His Tâoist masters told him that "among all the spirits of heaven, the highest in rank was the one dwelling in the star T'âi-yî (in Draco); that the five heavenly rulers were on his left; and that, in accordance with ancient custom on the part of the Head of the State, he should sacrifice to T'âi-yî."[1] Wû, otherwise a powerful ruler, was so infatuated about these men, that he complied with their request. He believed in their astrology, as he did in their alchemy, their herb and elixir of immortality, their stories about Immortals, and their communications with spiritual beings.

The origin of the present Tâoism.

5. We are now in a position to understand, so far as such a subject can be understood, the forms which a system so different from the views and worship of the state religion, as seen in Confucianism, assumed during the Han dynasty and the changes that it has subsequently undergone.

The superstitions that constitute the substance of the system were indigenous, and had

[1] See a Paper by Dr. Edkins in the "Companion to the Shanghâi Almanac," for 1857, on the Chinese worship of the Stars.

existed and been growing from a very early date. Our study in the first Lecture of a few of the primitive written characters showed us a belief in God, and even a monotheism, when they were formed; but there were at the same time ideas of which the outcome was likely to be Sabaism, and the traces of a system of divination were still more marked. Those tendencies to superstition could have been checked and corrected only by a healthy and general development of the doctrine of God; and this did to some extent take place. But the effect of it was marred by the restriction of the divine worship to the Head of the state as the representative of the people. Religious worship, as a power to invigorate piety and stimulate morality, was thus "cribbed, cabined, and confined." Men, debarred from communion with the Great Spirit, resorted more eagerly to inferior spirits, to the spirits of their fathers, and to spirits generally. One passage in the Shû King, referring to a very early time, not later certainly than that of the sage Shun, speaks of "communications between earth and heaven, and descents (of spirits),"[1] which required the interference of government. The accredited worship of ancestors, with that of the departed great added to it, was

---

[1] The Shû, V. xxvii. ch. i.

not enough to satisfy the cravings of men's minds. They wanted to have to do with spirits, not as paying to them the cold tributes of filial piety and admiration, but as receiving from them what they were supposed to be able to impart according to the activity of their nature. As a contemporary of Confucius, trying to explain the passage of the Shû to which I have just alluded, said, "The people intruded into the functions of the regulators of the spirits and their worship. They abandoned their duties to their fellow-men, and tried to bring down spirits from above. The spirits themselves, no longer kept in check and subjected to rule, made their appearance irregularly and disastrously."[1] In this explanation there was superstitious error on the part of the statesman who offered it; but it shows what was the natural result of the relation between the Chinese people and the religious constitution of their country.

Position of Confucius to the growing Tâoism of his time.

There is no doubt that for two thousand years many fantastic and gross superstitions

[1] "Narratives of the States"; see Chinese Classics, II. 593, 594.

had been growing in China, when Confucius appeared upon its stage. And the position which he took up in regard to them is very characteristic of the man. I drew attention in my last Lecture to his advice to "respect the spirits but to keep aloof from them," which has been objected to as showing the non-religious-ness of his nature; but we receive a different impression from it when we know what the latent Tâoism of his day was. Both it, and the other saying that "to sacrifice to a spirit with whom one has no proper connexion was flattery," were directed against the superstition that was by-and-by to have so portentous a development. Again, the first of the four sub-jects on which he eschewed conversation was "extraordinary things." The account I have given you of the emperor Wû of Han shows of what character those extraordinary things were. The sage evidently thought that super-stition was best combated by taking no notice of it,—that speech might be silvern, but silence was golden. There are times when that is the case. I do not think Confucius' time was one of them. Nor was he the man in whom silence was justifiable when the interests of truth were concerned.

Rapid degeneracy after Confucius.

After the death of Confucius, the intellectual and social degeneracy of the nation went on more rapidly. The picture which Mencius draws of its state in the fourth and third centuries B.C. is frightful. " Unemployed scholars indulged in unreasonable discussions." Heresiarchs were numerous. Mencius did his best to hold up the standard of Confucian truth. Lieh-tsze before him, and Chwang-tsze, his contemporary, were not afraid to ridicule the master. Dr. Chalmers has happily said that they used him, as the Philistine lords used Samson, "to make sport for them." It is remarkable that Mencius does not mention these philosophers by name and enter the arena against them ; but it was probably their mockery of Confucius which made him pile together the opinions of others and himself that among mortal men there had never been that sage's equal.

From Mencius to the rise of the Han dynasty.

In the third century B.C. there occurred the death of Mencius, the extinction of the dynasty of Châu, the subjugation of all the feudal states amid "hideous ruin and combustion," and the establishment of the empire of Ch'in. We have seen already how the founder of that empire was a blind and devoted believer in Tâoist superstitions. His line happily terminated with his son. The foundations of the dynasty laid in the ground soft with the blood of millions of the people could not last longer. The Han empire dates from B.C. 206. The old Confucianism was at a low ebb. Its books had been burnt. Many of its most distinguished adherents had been buried alive. A reaction soon commenced, but the work of reconstruction was tedious. Though the founder of the Han visited the master's tomb in B.C. 194, and offered an ox in sacrifice to him, nearly two centuries elapsed before his first title as "the all-complete and illustrious" was conferred on him by the emperor P'ing. During all this time, Tâoism had the field very much to itself, and with what result we have seen in the history of the emperor Wû. The superstitions of more than 2000 years' existence came to a head and effloresced. Chang Tâo-ling attracted the imperial notice in the first century of our era ; and a popedom or patriarchate of the system has existed in the line of his descendants to the present day. With all this Tâoism was not then a religion, with temples, and liturgies, and forms of public

worship. It only became so after Buddhism
began to have free course in China. The
shaven representatives of Buddhism, and the
wearers of the "yellow caps"[1] of Tâoism—for
I do not like to call either the one class or the
other by the name of priests—are now constantly
seen associated in the same service, and repeated
attempts have been made to amalgamate them
into one class.[2] Though these were resisted on
both sides, yet Tâoism, in organizing the forms
of its worship and liturgies, borrowed more from
Buddhism than Buddhism did from it. Its professors, however, have always persisted, in opposition to Buddhism, and in spite of the efforts of
the Government, in refusing to submit to the
yoke of celibacy.

[1] Dr. Chalmers says : "They are called Yellow Caps,
because they wear the style of caps instituted by Hwang
Tî, the Yellow Tî." But the thing made of yellow wood,
and helping to bind up the hair in a knot, can hardly be
called "a cap." I had one for years in my possession,
—given to me by its owner on his receiving Christian
baptism. "Top" would be a better name for it ; crown
is a term of too much dignity.

[2] It is related, for instance, in the "General Mirror of
History," under A.D. 555, that the emperor of the Ch'î
dynasty, that there might no longer be two systems,
commanded all "the Yellow Tops" to become shaven
Shamans. Some of them refusing, it is said, four were
put to death, and there was a general compliance with
the decree !"

Connexion of Tâoism with what are called the State gods.

6. When Confucianism was the sole religion of China, there was no idolatry in it ; and while the name of Tî or God has been given by the Buddhists to Indra, and perhaps to other Indian deities,[1] and there are multitudes of Tâoist idols who are called gods, great gods, and supreme gods, an image has never been fashioned of the god of the old classics. Indeed, it was not till after the image of Buddha was brought to the capital, in A.D. 65, that images or statues of Confucius and other great men of the past began to be made.

But when Tâoism and Buddhism had made good their footing in the empire, and were recognized by the Government, it was possible to multiply idol-deities indefinitely, and this has been done in what are called the state gods. Of these the three principal are the fathers of Medicine (for Fû-hsî and two others

---

[1] Dr. Medhurst, in his "Dissertation on the Theology of the Chinese," pp. 248, 249, says, "In the Buddhistic classic, Chăng Tâo Chî, we have Tî, frequently prefixed to Shih, and used in the sense of the God Shih Kia-mun-a." But Tî Shih is the God Indra (Shakra). I do not know that the name is given to Shakyamuni or Gautama Buddha.

are associated under this name), Kwan Yü (a hero of our third century, the most likeable character in the famous romance known as "The History of the Three Kingdoms"), the god of war, a special favourite of the Manchû emperors; and Wăn-ch'ang, the god of litera- ture, a star deity, whose seat is in a constellation which forms part of Ursa Major. Wăn-ch'ang is a dangerous rival to Confucius as the patron of literature, and Kwan-Tî was in 1856 appointed to receive the same divine honours of worship that are given to the sage, because the year before he had manifested himself, and made the imperial troops grandly successful in an engage- ment with the T'âi-p'ings. And it was not the first time that he had appeared turning the tide of battle, as Castor and Pollux did for the Romans at Lake Regillus. A special officer, representing the emperor, with a suite of atten- dants, repairs to the temples of these deities twice a year, and on behalf of the emperor presents the appointed offerings and reads the prayers.

But while these are the principal state gods, the number of others less exalted is very great. It was said to Judah of old time, "According to the number of thy cities are thy gods;" and much more than this is true of China. The cities and smaller towns all have their tutelary deities, which are appointed by the government, and the local authorities render the imperial homage at the set times. The number of deities and temples, moreover, increases every year, for the pope does not canonize on so large a scale as the emperor of China. Now the temples of all the state gods are in the hands of the ministers of Tâoism ; and if you would see the system in its glory, or rather in its shame, you must visit the temple of the tutelary deity of one of the provincial capitals. If your choice has fallen on a good day for the visit, the place is crowded with worshippers and loungers. There are astrologers, diviners, geomancers, physiognomists, *et id genus omne*, all plying their trades, or waiting to be asked to do so. Each shrine has its visitors and suppliants. The whole place is grimy, and the air is loaded with odours that are anything but perfumes from Araby the blessed. There, too, you shall see in "the chamber of Horrors" frightful representations of the punishments of Hades,—of what is being transacted in the courts of the other world.

The moral teaching of Tâoism.

7. But I will not enter on any description of these until I have first given you some idea of

the moral teaching of the system. This is communicated to the public for the most part in what we should call tracts or pamphlets, pubblished as exhortations under the name of the state gods and other deities. They contain a great deal of good advice derived from the Confucian books, with an intermixture of what is queer and grotesque. The most popular and characteristic of all the Tâoist practical works is "The Book of Actions and their Retributions,"[1] ascribed to "The most High," which is commonly taken as meaning Lâo-tsze. The name of the treatise, however, occurs first in a catalogue of the Sung dynasty. The writer was familiar with the ethics of Confucianism and Buddhism as well as those of his own religion; and while the teaching of the latter predominates, there is nothing contrary to the doctrines of the other two. Commencing with the general statement that "There are no special doors (in men's lot) for calamity and blessing, which come as

---

[1] This treatise was all translated, with many illustrative anecdotes, by the late Stanislas Julien, and several versions in English have since appeared, done from Julien's version more than from the original text. Julien rendered the title by "Le Livre des Récompenses et des Peines." That which I have given is more correct, but "Actions" must be taken as including thoughts and purposes though unacted.

men themselves call them, and that their recompenses follow good and evil, as the shadow follows the substance," the treatise says that there are spirits which take note of men's transgressions, and according to their lightness or gravity, curtail the term of life. Several of those spirits are then enumerated, some whose seat is in the stars, three that reside in the human body, and the spirit of the furnace. The last four on certain days go up to the court of heaven, and report the results of their observation. Great transgressions cost a man twelve years of life, and small ones a hundred days.

After this preamble there follows the description of a good man, one whose characteristics would make us all acknowledge that he should be called such; and the result to him is that "Men respect him, and Heaven protects him, and Spirits defend him, and whatsoever he does shall prosper;—he may hope to become an Immortal." If he be ambitious to be "an Immortal of heaven," he must give the proof of thirteen hundred good deeds. If he be content to be "an Immortal of earth," three hundred will suffice.

There is then given at much greater length the description of a bad man. More than two hundred traits of character are stated, which we should all condemn more or less severely. Others had better have been omitted, and several are wrong only because they are contrary to the superstitions of the system. A man, *e.g.*, must not sing and dance on the last day of the moon or of the year; must not shout and get into a passion on the first day of the moon or in the morning; must not weep, spit, or be guilty of other indecency towards the north; must not sigh, sing, or cry in front of the furnace; must not spit at a shooting star, point at a rainbow, or look long at the sun or moon.

In the case of crimes such as are enumerated, the spirit in charge of the perpetrator's life, according to a righteous decision, takes away from his appointed time periods of twelve years or of a hundred days. When the term of life is exhausted, death ensues. If at death there still remain guilt unpunished, the judgment extends to his posterity.

Finally, the treatise thus concludes: "When one's mind is directed to good, though the good be not yet done, the good spirits are in attendance on him; and when one's mind is directed to evil, though the evil be not yet done, the bad spirits are in attendance on him.

"If he has done the wicked thing, and afterwards alters his way, and repents, not doing anything wicked, but endeavouring to do everything that is good, after a time he will obtain good fortune and prosperity: this is what is called changing calamity into blessing.

"The words, looks, and deeds of the good man are all good. If all the three are seen to be so every day, after three years Heaven will surely send down blessing on him. And the words, looks, and deeds of the bad man are all evil. If all the three are seen to be so every day, after three years Heaven will surely send down calamity on him. Should you not exert yourself to do what is good?"

Such is a specimen of the moral teaching of Tâoism. You can form your own judgment of it. One sentence which I quoted says that "If at death there still remain guilt unpunished, the judgment extends to the culprit's posterity." This is the view of retribution of which I spoke in my second lecture on Confucianism,—that it works itself out for good or ill in the descendants of the individual. If he himself have any punishment to receive after this present life, Confucianism says nothing about it. And the author of "Actions and their Retributions" was equally silent.

The purgatory and hell of Tâoism.

8. But since he wrote, Tâoism has received a new and frightful development, which in great measure has come to it from Buddhism quite as evidently as its doctrine of a Trinity or the three Holy Ones. It is the belief in transmigration in its grossest form, made still more gross in the process of its adaptation. The Tâoist is now called on to believe in a purgatory, consisting of ten courts of Justice situated at the bottom of a great ocean which lies down in the depths of the earth. Pictures of the punishments inflicted in these courts are exhibited in the temple of the spirit of "the Eastern Mountain," which forms a part of the temple of the greater tutelary deity of each provincial city, and receives consequently from foreigners the name of "The chamber of Horrors." A full account of this purgatory is contained in a work, of which a translation is given by Mr. Herbert A. Giles in an appendix to his "Strange Stories from a Chinese Studio," published only in January this year,[1] and I

---

[1] "Strange Stories from a Chinese Studio. Translated and Annotated by Herbert A. Giles, of H. M.'s Consular Service (Thomas De La Rue and Co.)." I had often wished that some one would take the trouble to translate all these stories. They are mainly Tâoist, though Bud-

freely avail myself of the results of his toil. The title of his original is—" The Divine Pano-rama, published by the mercy of Yü-Tî,[1] that men and women may repent them of their faults, and make atonement for their sins."

The description of the courts is preceded by a recital of which this is a part. "On the birth-day of the saviour P'û-sa,[2] as the spirits of purgatory were thronging round to offer their congratulations, the ruler of the infernal regions spake as follows :—' My wish is to release all souls, and every moon, as this day comes round, I would wholly or partially remit the punishment of erring shades, and give them life once more in one of the six Paths.[3]

dhism and Buddhist monks frequently appear. If we had only an equal collection of the "extraordinary things" about which Confucius wòuld not speak !

[1] This may be called the Tâoist seal on the document. Yü-Tî is the Yü Hwang Shang Tî of p. 169.

[2] P'û-sa is an abbreviated form of the Chinese characters for the Sanskrit Bodhisattva, meaning one whose essence has become intelligence, and who has only once more to pass through human existence before he attains to Buddhaship (Eitel). The name is entirely Buddhistic, but it is used in Chinese generally for a deity. The P'û-sa here would seem to be the ruler of the Infernal Regions.

[3] The six gâti, or paths of transmigration, the six con-ditions of sentient existence : devas, men, asuras, beings in hell, prêtas, and animals. The last three of these conditions are the "three States "subsequently mentioned.

But alas ! the wicked are many, and the virtuous
few. Nevertheless the punishments in the dark
region are too severe, and require some modification. Any wicked soul that repents and
induces one or two others to do likewise shall
be allowed to set this off against the punishments which should be inflicted.' The judges
of the ten Courts then agreed that all who lead
virtuous lives from their youth upwards shall
be escorted at their death to the land of the
Immortals ; that all whose balance of good
and evil is exact shall escape the bitterness of
the three States, and be born again among
men ; that those who have repaid their debts
of gratitude and friendship, and fulfilled their
destiny, yet have a balance of evil against
them, shall pass through the various courts of
purgatory, and then be born again among men,
rich, poor, old, young, diseased or crippled, to
be put a second time upon trial. Then, if they
behave well, they may enter into some happy
state ; but if badly, they will be dragged by
horrid devils through all the courts, suffering
bitterly as they go, and will again be born,
to endure in life the uttermost of poverty and
wretchedness, in death the everlasting tortures
of hell." There follows a good deal of explanation, but this relaxation of the severity of the

punishments, thus agreed upon by the judges
of the ten Courts, was approved by the ruling
P'û-sa, and then on a certain day submitted
by the whole eleven of them to Yü-Tî. Yü-Tî
also approved and said, "Good! Good! Henceforth let all spirits take note of any mortal
who vows to lead a virtuous life, and, repenting,
promises to sin no more. Two punishments
shall be remitted to him. And if, in addition
to this, he succeeds in doing five virtuous acts,
then he shall escape all punishment and be
born again in some happy state;—if a woman,
she shall be born as a man. But more than five
virtuous acts shall enable such a soul to obtain
the salvation of others, and redeem wife and
family from the tortures of hell. Let these
regulations be published in the Divine Panorama, and circulated on earth by the spirits of
the City Guardian."

Thus ends the preamble of the account of the
courts of purgatory. We see the lenient constitution under which men are placed since the
meetings in purgatory and heaven, which the
document describes, were held,—placed with
regard to the purgatory and hell in the future!
The day and month in which the Powers of
purgatory laid their counsels before Yü-Tî in
heaven are stated, but not the year. I shall be

anxious to know what it was, and also whether the publication is guaranteed by the Heavenly Master Chang, the pope of Tâoism on earth, as well as by Yü Hwang, its God in heaven. But with this document in circulation, Dr. Edkins did well to speak as he did at the Missionary Conference in Shanghâi in 1877 :—" Among statements which I made years ago and have now to correct as imperfect or erroneous is this, that the Tâoists have no hell, but only a heaven."

After the preamble of which I have spoken there follows a description of each of the ten courts of purgatory, with their punishments and the crimes for which these are inflicted. The ninth court, for instance, presided over by His Infernal Majesty, P'ing Tăng, is a vast, circular gehenna, many leagues in breadth, enclosed by an iron net, and subdivided into sixteen wards. " In the first the wicked souls have their bones beaten and their bodies scorched. In the second, their muscles are drawn out and their bones rapped. In the third, ducks eat their heart and liver. In the fourth, dogs eat their intestines and lungs. In the fifth, they are splashed with hot oil. In the sixth, their heads are crushed in a frame, and their tongues and teeth are drawn out. In the seventh, their

13

brains are taken out and their skulls filled
with hedgehogs.   In the eighth, their heads
are steamed and their brains scraped.   In the
ninth, they are dragged about by sheep till
they drop to pieces.   In the tenth, they are
squeezed in a wooden press and pricked on
the head.   In the eleventh, their hearts are
ground in a mill.   In the twelfth, boiling water
drips on to their bodies.   In the thirteenth,
they are stung by wasps.   In the fourteenth,
they are tortured by ants and maggots; they
are then stewed and finally wrung out (like
clothes).   In the fifteenth, they are stung by
scorpions.   In the sixteenth, they are tortured
by venomous snakes, crimson and scarlet."

Sed ohe! jam satis.   I will not weary you
with more of the horrible details of the " Divine
Panorama."   I have quoted from it so largely,
that there might be no doubt as to the recent
development of a purgatory and hell in the
system of Tâoism.   The impulse leading to
that development was derived evidently in
the first place from Buddhism.   But for the
Indian belief in metempsychosis or transmigration, the Tâoists would never have fashioned their
courts of purgatory; but I am not aware
that Buddhism maintains an unending suc-
cession of transmigrations; and still less that

when transmigration has done its best and there is no good result, there is afterwards an everlasting hell to which irremediable souls are consigned. This seems to be a tenet peculiar to Táoism, that the soul must live on for ever in its individuality. A sentence of the preamble, which I did not quote above, deals with the unbelief of many who say that "when a man dies, there is an end of him ; that, when he has lost his skin (that is, in Shakspearian phrase, 'shuffled off this mortal coil'), he has already suffered the worst that can befal him ; that living men can be tortured, but no one ever saw a man's ghost in the pillory; that after death all is unknown, and so on." In reply to such unbelievers it is said, "Truly these men do not know that the body alone perishes, but the soul lives for ever and ever; and that whatsoever evil they do in this life, the same will be done to them in the life to come." Táoism perhaps derived this tenet from some Christian source ; it certainly teaches in the "Divine Panorama" the everlasting existence and misery of the irreclaimably bad. But it says also that some get to be "Immortals" without passing through the fires of purgatory, and others who, after being subjected to them, have conducted themselves aright in a new and transmigrated

life. Is their immortality also everlasting ? I
presume the system would say so, though no
texts occur to me that expressly affirm it, or
speak of any advance in eternity from one
degree of brightness and happiness to another
and higher.

Tâoism as a magical power in conflict with malevolent spirits.

10. I must bring my description of Tâoism
as a religion to a close ; and in order to do so,
I withdraw with you from the shades of the
infernal world, and return to the realm of light
and mortal life. But the system seems to dog
our steps, and to let loose millions of malevolent
spirits to trouble and afflict us. Though we see
them not, hosts of them may be all about us,
seeking opportunity to inflict various injury.
They may assume the forms of snakes and
foxes, of men and women, and entrap the unwary.
Or they may take demoniac possession of their
victims, and produce pining sickness, mooning
melancholy, and wild frenzy. They haunt
houses, and frequent thickets. Their sounds,
weird and eerie, are heard in the darkness of
the night, when the wind is howling about the
roof, or the rats and mice are holding revel on
the floor, or behind the wainscot in the crevices

of the walls. The dread of spirits is the night-
mare of the Chinaman's life, and to this dread
Tâoism panders. It encourages it by its teachings, and lives in a great measure by it. This
is the prevailing characteristic of the system at
the present day.

My impression is that the alchemy which was
cultivated in the Han dynasty pretty well wore
itself out in five or six centuries. The quest for
the herb and preparation of the pill of immortality held their ground longer. The writer of
the popular paraphrase of "The sacred Edict"
appeals to his hearers against the good doctors
of Tâo, who, in the deep recesses and caves of
their mountains, occupy themselves with refining
the vital spirit, and talk about becoming Immortals. "Who," he asks, "ever saw them fly up
into the air in broad daylight? Their preten-
sions are a farce." But while other superstitions
may have been modified in the course of time,
that about the existence of spirits and their
interference with men is as powerful now as
ever it was, and from the pope or Heavenly
Master downwards, every "yellow Top" is
gifted in consequence with the powers of a
magician, who with charms and liturgies fights
against the malevolent demons. Of course no
one is equal to the pope. The sword that has

come down from our first century is very powerful. He can even imprison the spirits, and it
is said that about his residence on the Lung-hû
mountain there are thousands of jars in rows, all
tenanted by demons whom the great magician
has shut up in them.

But every member of the order has his own
ability, and makes more or less by writing
charms and preparing amulets. The charms
are figures, and characters, single or combined,
drawn and written in grotesque forms. The
myriads of doors on which you see them pasted
shows the thriving trade that their writers must
have. A few years ago, over a large extent of
the country, men were startled by the sudden
and unaccountable disappearance of their tails
or long cues. An invasion of cholera could not
have frightened the people more. It was the
work of malevolent spirits! There was a run
upon the charm-manufactories. It was thought
that four characters, mysteriously woven together
and wrapped up in the cue, warded the spirits off.

Tâoism thus becomes at times dangerous to
the peace of the community. Its adherents will
generally be found making common cause against
foreigners with the literati. Both fear the advance
of science and general knowledge, as threatening
their prestige and their means of living; and in

the populace, inflamed by Tâoist superstitions, a scheming scholar will find, not a host that will take arms against its own government or foreign soldiers, but a mob that in blind fury will commit the most frightful deeds of violence and outrage.

Geomancy and the worship of the dead.

11. The only other features of Tâoism which I think it necessary to mention are the superstition of geomancy, and the views which it teaches the people to take of their departed relatives, and the duties to be paid to them. And even on these two features I can touch but slightly ;—to treat exhaustively of geomancy would require more than one lecture for itself. The common name for the thing in Chinese is făng-shui, "wind and water." Dr. Yates says that "it is never used except with reference to the repose of the dead, or the influence of the dead upon the happiness and welfare of the living."[1] I would extend this account of it, for it has to do with the selection of sites for the habitations of the living, as well as of graves for the dead. The aim of the Tâoists, however, is

[1] Yates's Paper on Ancestral Worship at the Conference in Shanghâi.

especially to provide the proper spots for the
graves. Only adepts in the system can be
relied on to do this, and large sums are often
paid for their services. If a coffin be interred
in an improper spot, the spirit of the dead is
made unhappy, and avenges itself by causing
sickness and other calamities to the relatives who
have not taken sufficient care for its repose. I
have known bodies kept unburied, lying in their
large and carefully cemented coffins, for a long
time, from the difficulty of selecting the best
site for the grave. I have known great excite-
ment and expenditure in connexion with the
removal of a coffin from a grave which had
turned out unpropitious, to one that was likely
to enable its tenant to rest in peace, and leave
his family circle unmolested.

With regard to the dead whose graves have
been selected in harmony with geomantic
principles, Tâoism teaches that each one has
three souls, one of which remains with the
corpse, and one with the spirit-tablet, while
the third is carried off to the purgatory, of
which I gave you some description a little ago.
Offerings must be presented at the grave,
before the spirit tablet, and in the temple of
the tutelary deity of the city. Special services,
often very expensive, may be held also either

by Buddhist monks or by Tâoist, or by both together as I have often seen, to deliver the soul from purgatory. Whether, when the deliverance has been in any case effected, the three souls are then reunited for an ascent to the region of the Immortals, or for a new career of trial upon earth,—that I have never found discussed in any Tâoist book that I have read. But what a falling off in these services to the dead, and the fear of calamity if they be not performed, from the Confucian worship of ancestors, and the filial piety of which it is represented as the fulfilment! To serve its own mercenary purposes, Tâoism seems to convert the souls of all the dead into malevolent spirits, and to cause what is done by their descendants for them to be done from fear and not from love.

I have done with the religion of Tâoism. Much research is still required from Chinese scholars to make clear everything connected with it and trace the process of its development, so as to satisfy the critical inquirer. But I am satisfied that I have given its general attributes fairly. It is not an ancient religion like that followed, illustrated, and transmitted by Confucius. It was begotten by Buddhism out of the old Chinese superstitions. Its forms are

those of Buddhism ; but its voice and spirit
are from its mother-superstitions, fantastic, base,
and cruel.   I have thought while setting it forth
of Milton's description of sin :—

> " The other shape,
> If shape it might be called, that shape had none
> Distinguishable in member, joint, or limb ;
> Or substance might be called that shadow seemed ;
> For each seemed either.   Black it stood as night,
> Fierce as ten furies, terrible as hell,
> And shook a dreadful dart."

It has proved too strong for Confucianism,
though acknowledging to a great extent the
social system and duties enjoined by the sage;
the government, holding only Confucianism
to be orthodox, has yet been compelled to
recognize and endow it, as well as Buddhism ;
it will long rage against the progress of Christianity.   But the more that the truths of real
science are disseminated in China, the weaker
will be the hold of Tâoism.   A time must come
when its errors will exist only in dark corners
and benighted minds, as is the case in Christendom with the alchemy, astrology, palmistry,
belief in witchcraft, and other superstitions
which long tried to maintain themselves even in
the Christian church.

Tâoism as a philosophy.

12. We must turn now to Tâoism as a philosophy. After I have done my best to describe it to you, so far as I profess to know it myself, you may think that a humbler name than philosophy would have been more suitable for it; but the discussion will not come to so lame and impotent a conclusion as the consideration of the religion has done. What I have to attempt is to give you some idea of the contents of the Tâo Teh King, which is our only text-book in the case. No other writing has come down to us from the pencil of Lâo-tsze, its author. It will not take long to put you in possession of everything about him that claims to rest on a historical foundation.

Historical account of Lâo-tsze.

13. Lâo-tsze is, probably, a title of respect, equivalent to "the Old or Venerable Philosopher." The two characters may also be translated " Old Boy," and it is a popular fancy that the philosopher was so called, because he was not born till his mother had carried him in her womb seventy-two years, or, according to some accounts, eighty-one years. No wonder that the child should have had white hair,—an " old

boy " of about fourscore years! That, of course, is an extravagant legend, and is found among a mass of similar stuff in the " Record of Spirits and Immortals " by Ko Hung, a writer of our fourth century, between nine hundred and a thousand years after the birth of our subject. Sze-mâ Ch'ien, however, commences a brief record of his life with this title, which must therefore have been in common use in the second century B.C. His surname was Lî, and his name *R*, meaning " ear," which gave place after his death to Tan, meaning "Flat-eared;" from which we may conclude that there was some peculiarity in the form of his ears. His birthplace was in the east of what is now the province of Ho-nan, and he was one of the Sze, " Recorders," or Historiographers," at the royal court of Châu, his special charge being that of a librarian.[1] In the year B.C. 517, as we saw, Confucius visited

---

[1] Lâo-tsze was in charge of the tsang shih, "the storehouse," or "house of deposit." In 1861 I interpreted this as meaning that he was "a treasury-keeper." Julien made him "keeper of the archives." Professor Douglas has met with a statement that Confucius visited him "to hand him a book to be placed in the archives (Confucianism and Tâoism, p. 176)." Chû Hsî says that Lâo-tsze was in charge of the tien-tsî and shû-tsî, "Canons and Records," or generally "Writings." Some make the " Canons " to have been those of the three lines of sovereigns before Fû-hsî!

the capital, his object, according to Ch'ien, being to make inquiries of Lâo-tsze on the subject of ceremonies. Whether this were the motive of the sage's journey or not, the two men then met. " Those whom you talk about," said Lâo-tsze to the other, " are dead, and their bones are mouldered to dust;—only their words are left. Moreover, when the superior man gets his time he mounts aloft; but, when the time is against him, he moves as if his feet were entangled. I have heard that a good merchant, though he has rich treasures deeply stored, appears as if he were poor, and that the superior man, though his virtue is complete, is yet to outward seeming stupid. Put away your proud air and many desires, your insinuating habit and wild will. These are of no advantage to you ;—this is all that I have to tell you." Confucius at this time was thirty-five years old, and Lâo-tsze was eighty-eight, if his birth, as is commonly believed, took place in B.C. 604. The difference of their age may be pleaded as justifying the style that Lâo-tsze employed in addressing his visitor. Confucius is made to say, after the interview, to his disciples, " I know how birds can fly, fishes swim, and animals run. But the runner may be snared, the swimmer hooked, and the flyer shot by the arrow. But there is the

dragon ;—I cannot tell how he mounts on the
wind through the clouds and rises to heaven.
To-day I have seen Lâo-tsze, and can only
compare him to the dragon."[1]

Ch'ien adds, " Lâo-tsze cultivated the tâo
and virtue, the chief aim of his studies being
how to keep himself concealed and remain unknown. He continued to reside at (the capital
of) Châu, but, after a long time, seeing the
decay of the dynasty, he left it, and went away
to the gate leading out of the state on the
north-west. Yin Hsî, keeper of the gate, said
to him, 'You are about to withdraw yourself
out of sight : I pray you to compose for me
(first) a book.' On this Lâo-tsze wrote a book
in two parts, setting forth his views on Tâo and
virtue, in more than five thousand characters.
He then went away, and it is not known where
he died. He was a superior man who liked to
keep himself unknown."

Ch'ien finally traces Lào-tsze's descendants
down to the beginning of the first century B.C.,
and concludes by saying, " Those who attach
themselves to the doctrine of Lâo-tsze condemn

[1] Then did the practice of calling Lî *R* Lâo-tsze originate
with Confucius ? If so, the sage would have reference in
the title to Lî's great age, and the reverence due to him
in consequence.

that of the literati, and the literati on their part condemn Lâo-tsze, verifying the saying, ' Parties, whose principles are different, cannot take counsel together.' Li *R* taught that transformation as a matter of course follows the doing nothing (to bring it about), and rectification in the same way ensues from being pure and still."

This morsel is all that we have of historical narrative about Lâo-tsze. There is nothing in it to make us think that he was more than a man of superior character, devoted to the study of the tâo and of virtue. There is no reason for us to doubt that the book which he wrote at the request of Yin Hsî, and for his special benefit in the first place, was the Tâo Teh King, which we still possess. The students of the tâo had in the time of Sze-mâ Ch'ien become a school distinct from the adherents of the orthodox Confucianism, and opposed to and by them. But there is no account of Lâo-tsze's deification, nothing of his pre-existence, and nothing of his travelling to the west and learning there doctrines which he embodied in his work. He goes through the pass out of the royal domain, alone, unattended ; and nothing more was ever heard of him.

Doubts have been thrown on the interview

between him and Confucius, and I do not accept
it myself with entire confidence. Allowing it,
however, to be true, there is a remarkable
similarity between the position and language of
Lâo-tsze in it and those of the recluses that
come before us in the Analects. They rate the
sage much as he did for not withdrawing from
the world altogether, and deride him for his
unceasing attempts, " hoping against hope," to
arrest the degenerate tendencies of the time.[1]
But for the Tâo Teh King, Lâo-tsze would have
been to us simply as one of them. Confucius
saw as clearly as he that, if things went on as
they were doing, the kingdom of Châu must
fall ;[2] but he said, " If right principles prevailed through the land, there would be no
need for my services." A sense of duty kept
him at his post, while Lâo-tsze and the others
abandoned the struggle and withdrew into
obscurity. I will make no further reference,
however, to Ch'ien's brief narrative, nor to
the legends, drawn for the most part from
the legend of Gautama Buddha,[3] but will call
your attention to the Tâo Teh King.

[1] Ana. XVIII. vi.
[2] Confucianism and Tâoism, p. 178.
[3] See note D.

Errors in the interpretation of the Tâo Teh King.

14. The preceding narrative would seem to fix the preparation of this treatise after the year B.C. 517. Containing but few more than five thousand characters,[1] it is about twice as long as the " Sermon on the Mount," though a good translation in English will take more space, owing to the condensed style of the original. It ought not to be difficult to analyse thoroughly so short a piece, and determine the meaning of its several chapters, but experience proves the reverse. Both native commentators and foreigners have been forward to acknowledge how hard it is to open the shell and bring out the meaning of the text. And the errors into which some scholars of great attainments and with the best intentions have fallen, in regard to some of its most important chapters, show us with what accuracy and caution our study of it should be prosecuted. I will illustrate this by two or three instances.

i. Father Prémare and other Roman Catholic missionaries about the beginning of last century made it their object to find in the old books of

---

[1] In the T'âi Shang hwun yüan Tâo Teh Chăn King, published at Shanghâi, I have counted 5330 characters.

China passages on which they could insist as in wonderful harmony with the teaching of our sacred scriptures. They did so especially in the Tâo Teh King. Montucci of Berlin, a partizan of their school of interpretation, writing on "Chinese Studies" in 1808, said, "Many things about a Triune God are so clearly expressed in it, that no one who has read this book can doubt that the mystery of the Most Holy Trinity was revealed to the Chinese five centuries before the coming of Jesus Christ."[1] I need hardly say that there is nothing in Lâo-tsze's work which can be wrested into a declaration of the Christian doctrine of the Trinity.

ii. Father Amiot, however, thought that he found such a passage in the first paragraph of the fourteenth chapter ;—to him there appeared in it the three persons of the Trinity. He translated it thus :—"He who is as it were visible and cannot be seen is called Khî (should be Î) ; he whom we cannot hear and who does not speak to the ears is called Hî; he who is as it were tangible, but whom we cannot touch, is called Weî."

It was reserved for Rémusat to outdo Amiot in his study of this text. A very considerable

[1] See Julien's Translation of the Tâo Teh King, Itrodnuction, p. iv.

Chinese scholar, and the first occupant of a
Chinese chair in Europe, he found the Hebrew
word Je-ho-va in the three syllables Î, hî, weî ;
and he published in 1823 his " Memoir on the
Life and Opinions of Lâo-tsze," to make known
and vindicate his discovery. All Europe was
startled by it. To find a Hebrew word,—the
great and incommunicable name of God,—in a
Chinese writing of the sixth century B.C.: how had
the name been carried to the east? what a part
might not the Tâo Teh King yet play in the
christianization of China! I became acquainted
with the view in 1838 from one of archbishop
Wiseman's Lectures on the "Connexion between
Science and Religion," and bought a copy of
Rémusat's memoir; I studied it during my
voyage to the east in 1839, and for two or three
years, whenever there was occasion to use the
name Jehovah in Chinese tracts issued under
my superintendence, it was represented by the
three syllables Î-hî-wei. The delusion did not
last long. When Julien's translation of the Tâo
Teh King, published in 1842, in which he exposed the error of his predecessor in the Chinese
chair, came into my hands, I was prepared to
agree with him.

The whole fourteenth chapter may be translated as follows. It is a favourable specimen

of the contents of the book. "We look at it, and do not see it : it is named the colourless. We listen for it, and do not hear it : it is named the soundless. We (try to) grasp it, and do not get hold of it : it is named the incorporeal. With these three qualities it cannot be investigated and defined ; and hence we blend them together and form a unity.

"Its upper part is not bright ; its lower part is not obscure. Ceaseless in its action, it (yet) cannot be named. (Finally) it returns, and again becomes nothing. This is what is called the form of what is formless, the image of the invisible. This is what is called being incapable of determination.

"We meet it, but we do not see its front ; we follow it, but we do not see its back parts. When we grasp the Tâo that was of old so as to deal with the existences of the present, and are able to know the old beginnings, this is what is called having the clue of Tâo."

The writer in all this was speaking of his Tâo, and not of any personal being. Many of his expressions are remarkable and tantalizing. They promise to conduct us to the brink of a grand prospect, and then there is before us but a sea of mist. If Lâo-tsze found it thus difficult to express his own idea of Tâo, it is not to be marvelled at, that students of his book, nearly 2500 years after him, should shrink from the attempt to define it.

iii. In his fourth lecture on "the Science of Religion" (pp. 249, 250), professor Max Müller quotes the greater part of the twenty-fifth chapter of the Tâo Teh King as an instance of the exalted character of the teachings to be found in the sacred books of other religions besides our own. The first sentence of his version is, "There is an infinite Being, which existed before heaven and earth." The sequel shows clearly that this being was the Tâo, Lâo-tsze's great theme. Of course professor Müller was translating from Julien's French version of the original, and that misled him as to the word "being," instead of "thing." Julien says, "Il est un être confus;" but when "confus" is exchanged for the English "infinite," we get too high an idea of the thought that was in the mind of Lâo-tsze. The verb, moreover, should be translated in the past tense.[1] The whole of the chapter is this:—"There was something chaotic and complete before the birth of heaven and earth. How still it was and

[1] Dr. Chalmers' version of the sentence is,—" There was something chaotic in nature which existed before heaven and earth."

formless, standing alone, and undergoing no change ; proceeding everywhere, and in no danger (of being exhausted) ! It may be regarded as the mother of all things.

" I do not know its name, but designate it the Tâo[1] (the Way) ; and forcing myself to frame a name for it, I call it the Great.

" Great, it passes on, in constant flux ; so passing on, it becomes remote ; when remote, it comes back.

" Therefore Tâo is great ; Heaven is great ; Earth is great ; the (sage) King is also great. In the circle of being there are four that are great, and the (sage) King is one of them.

" The (sage) man has for his law the earth ; the earth has heaven for its law ; heaven has Tâo for its law ; and the law of Tâo is its own spontaneity."

Things that are taught in the book.

15. I have dwelt sufficiently on errors into which European scholars have fallen in their

---

[1] Chalmers says here ;—" I know not its name, but give it the title of Tâo." Julien's version is to the same effect. The term which they translate by " title," " entitle," is that indicating the name or designation given to a man in China on his marriage. What it is important to observe is this :—that Tâo is not the name of Lâo-tsze's subject, but a descriptive designation of it.

illustration of what is taught in the Tâo Teh King. I have ventured to point them out simply as a helpful preparation for our study of what the book does really teach. It is not without a feeling of the difficulty of the undertaking that I proceed to tell you some of the results to which such a study conducts us.

There are two translations of the work, whose merits I gladly acknowledge :—one by the late Stanislas Julien, published at Paris in 1842 ; and the other by the Rev. Dr. Chalmers of Canton, published here in London in 1868. I am in possession also of a version in German, by Victor von Strauss, published at Leipzig in 1870. There is a second and later version, also in German, by Reinhold von Plänckner, that I have not yet seen. During the last two years I have myself made two versions of the original, and advanced a considerable way with a third. Notwithstanding the succours afforded by Julien and Chalmers, I undertook the labour of translating afresh for myself, transcribing at the same time the original and the happiest portions of Chinese commentary on it, because I have learned by experience that such a process gives one most readily a mastery of the old books of China. Their meaning and spirit soak gradually into the mind. My long dealing with them has

not yet enabled me to make them throw open
their gates at the first summons.   After all my
pains with the Tâo Teh King I am still waiting
for more light on many chapters.   I think, however, I have attained to the practical drift and
aim of the old moralist and mystic.

i. Let us hear **what he says of himself** in
contrast with the majority of other men.

" If we could give up (constantly adding to)
our knowledge, we should have no anxieties.

" There is not much difference between the
Yes (with which we answer a question), and
the Yea (with which we give a flattering assent
to the views of others); but how far separate
are the good and evil (to which these responses
lead) !

" What all fear is indeed to be feared ; but
how immense is the number of things (which
our increasing knowledge will thus make us
fear) !

" All men look pleased, as if enjoying a full
banquet, as if mounted on a tower in spring.   I
alone am still and indifferent, my desires not
having yet shown themselves ;—I am like an
infant that has not yet smiled.   I look forlorn,
as if I had nowhere to go to.

" All others have enough and to spare ; I
alone look as if I had lost everything.

"My mind is that of a stupid man ; I am in a state of chaos.

"The common people look very intelligent ; I alone am very dark. The common people are full of discrimination ; I alone have none.

"I am drifted about as on the sea ; I am carried by the wind, as if I had nowhere to rest.

"All others have their amount of capacity ; I alone am stupid, like a rude borderer.

"(Thus) I alone am different from other men, and what I value is the nursing mother."[1]

The "nursing mother" is the Tâo, and in order to enjoy her care and nurture one must have the emptiness of mind and freedom from desires and ambitions which the writer describes as characteristic of himself.

ii. It is self-evident that **emptiness, or freedom from preoccupation, is a condition of receptivity** ; Lâo-tsze also teaches that such **emptiness is necessary to usefulness.** Take the following chapter in illustration of this :—
"The thirty spokes unite in the one nave ; but it is on the empty space (for the axle), that the use of the carriage depends. Clay is fashioned into vessels ; but it is on its empty hollowness that the use of a vessel depends. Doors and windows are cut out to form apart-

[1] Ch. 20.

ments, but it is on the empty space in them that the use of an apartment depends. Therefore what has a positive existence serves for profitable adaptation, and what has no positive existence for the actual use."[1]

iii. Both in the processes of nature, spoken of as the action of heaven and earth, and in the activities of man, **what corresponds to this emptiness is a freedom from all selfish motive, or purpose centering in self.** It is said, "The sage deals with affairs (as if) he were doing nothing, and performs his teaching without words. (In the same way, in nature), all things shoot up (in spring) without a word spoken, and grow (in summer) without a claim for their production. They go through their processes (in autumn) without any display of pride in them, and the results are realized, (in winter) without any assumption of ownership."[2]

So again: "Heaven and earth have no (purpose of) love (in bestowing their favours): they deal with all things as the dogs of straw (in sacrifice) are dealt with. The sages have no (purpose of) love (in their action); they deal with the people as the dogs of straw (in sacrifice) are dealt with.

[1] Ch. 11.   [2] Ch. 2.

" May not the space between heaven and earth be compared to the bellows of a forge? It becomes empty, and yet is not exhausted; it is moved (again), and sends forth air the more.

" Many words produce speedy exhaustion (of the breath); there is nothing like keeping that which is within."[1]

The book often speaks of doing nothing, desiring nothing, and so on, while the greatest results follow from the quietude; but in all such instances we are to understand "on purpose," or "with a motive." Thus it is said :—" States are ruled by (measures of) correction; war is carried on by craft; (but) it is only by doing nothing (with design) that the kingdom can be made one's own. Therefore the sages said, 'We will do nothing (with purpose), and the people will of themselves be transformed; we will love quietness, and the people will of themselves be rectified; we will take no measures, and the people will of themselves become rich; we will free ourselves from desire, and the people will of themselves become simple-minded.' "[2]

From the three points which I have stated we

---

[1] Ch. 5. " Figures of straw made like dogs " were used at services of prayer for rain, but after the service was over, they were of no account. The reference to them is not very happy. [2] Ch. 57.

begin to get an idea of the meaning of the word Tâo in the treatise. Of the three English terms that suggest themselves for it,—the Way, Reason, and the Word,[1]—the Way, in the sense of Method, is the one that is suitable.[2] Tâo is the style of action, which Lâo-tsze wished to recommend and inculcate,—action proceeding from a mind in a state of calm repose according to the spontaneity of its nature, without bias of partiality or hypocrisy. If Methodism and Methodist had not been so well appropriated in English, I should have recommended their employment for Tâoism and Tâoist.

iv. As might be expected from the above principles, **humility** has a distinguished place in the teachings of Lâo-tsze. He says:—" The incomplete becomes complete; the crooked

[1] Chalmers' Translation, p. xi.

[2] Professor Douglas (Confucianism and Tâoism, p. 189), in his careful account of the Tâo Teh King, says, " If we were compelled to adopt a single word to represent the Tâo of Lâo-tsze, we, should prefer the sense in which it is used by Confucius, ' the way,' that is μέθοδος." But there does not lie behind the name as Confucius uses it the same view of what constitutes the proper method. Ratio in Latin has also the meaning of method, and if the word rationalism carried in it that signification (which it does not), its use for Tâoism would not be objectionable.

becomes straight; the hollow becomes full; the worn out becomes new; he who desires little gets much; he who desires much goes astray.

"Therefore the sage holds (this) one thing (of humility) in his embrace, and is a pattern to the world. He is free from self-display, and so he shines; from self-assertion, and so he is distinguished; from boasting, and so his merit is acknowledged; from self-conceit, and so his superiority is allowed. It is because he is thus free from striving that therefore no one can strive with him.

"That saying of the ancients, that 'the incomplete becomes complete' was not vainly spoken. All real completion is comprehended in it." [1]

Water is a favourite emblem of the Tâo with the author. Thus he says:—"The highest goodness is like water. Water is good at benefiting all things; and without striving (to the contrary), it occupies the (low) place, which all men dislike. Hence its (nature) is near to that of Tâo. It is because it does not strive (against its natural tendency) that there is no murmuring against it.[2] And again:—"There is nothing in the world more supple and weak

[1] Ch. 2.   Ch. 8.

than water, and yet, for dealing with things
that are hard and strong, nothing can surpass
it : let no one try to change it for anything
else.   Every one in the world knows that the
soft overcomes the hard, and the weak the
strong, but none can carry it out in practice.
Therefore a sage has said, ' He who accepts
the reproach of a state becomes the lord of
its altars ; he who accepts the misfortunes of
his state becomes the king of all under
heaven.' "[1]

v. There are other chapters which I should
like to quote on the virtue of humility, but
the want of space and time compels me to
leave them out.   Hear our author on his **three
precious things.**

" All in the world say that my Tâo is great,
but that I seem to be inferior to others.   Now
it is just this greatness which makes me seem
inferior to others.   Those who are deemed
equal to others have long been—small men.

" But there are three precious things which I
prize and hold fast.   The first is gentle compassion ; the second is economy ; the third is
(humility), not presuming to take precedence in
the world.   With gentle compassion I can be
brave.   With economy I can be liberal.   Not

[1] Ch. 78.

presuming to claim precedence in the world, I can make myself a vessel fit for the most distinguished services. Now-a-days they give up gentle compassion, and cultivate (mere physical) courage ; they give up economy, and (try to be) lavish (without it) ; they give up being last, and seek to be first :—of all which the end is death.

"Gentle compassion is sure to overcome in fight, and to be firm in maintaining its own. Heaven will save its possessor, protecting him by his gentleness."[1]

vi. But there is in the Tâo Teh King something even higher and nobler than this. Lâo-Tsze had attained to the conception of **returning good for evil.** I give you the whole of the chapter in which he mentions that as an element of his system.

"(It is the way of Tâo) not to act from any personal motive ; to conduct affairs without feeling the trouble of them ; to taste without being aware of the flavour ; to account the great as small and the small as great ; to recompense injury with kindness.

"(The follower of Tâo) anticipates things that would become difficult while they are easy, and does things that would become great while they are little. The difficult things in the world

[1] Ch. 67.

arise from what are easy, and the great things
from what are small. Thus it is that the sage
never does what is great, and therefore can
accomplish the greatest things.

"He who assents lightly will be found to
keep but little faith. He who takes many
things easily is sure to meet with many difficulties. Hence the sage sees difficulty in (what
seem) easy things, and therefore never has any
difficulties."[1]

The sentiment about returning good for evil
was new in China, and originated with Lâo-tsze.
We saw in the second Lecture how Confucius
was consulted about it by some of his disciples
whose notice it had attracted. The sage, I am
sorry to say, was not able to take it in.

vii. There are other points of Lâo-tsze's teaching which I should like to bring before you,
but it is high time that the lecture came to
a close. **He seems to condemn the infliction
of capital punishment ;**[2] **and he deplores the
practice of war.**[3] **With the progress of
knowledge and society, however, as we think
and speak, he had no sympathy. He looked
back to an early time of Arcadian innocence
and enjoyment, and regretting that it had**

[1] Ch. 63.   [2] Chh. 73, 74.
          [3] Ch. 69.

passed away, would gladly have reproduced it on however small a scale. In his last chapter but one he says: "In a small state with a few inhabitants, (I would so order it that) the people, though supplied with all kinds of implements, would not (care to) use them; I would make them look on death as a most grievous thing, but not go away to a distance (to escape it). Though they had boats and carriages, they should have no occasion to ride in them. Though they had buff coats and sharp weapons, they should not don or use them. I would make them return to the use of knotted cords (instead of written characters). They should think their (coarse) food sweet, their (plain) clothing beautiful, their (poor) houses places of rest, and their common (simple) ways sources of enjoyment.

"There should be a neighbouring state within sight, and the sounds of the fowls and dogs should be heard from it to us without interruption, but I would make the people to old age, even to death, have no intercourse with it."

It is difficult to suppose that these sentences were written seriously. The thoughts are those of a hermit, and not of a philosopher. Would Lâo-tsze really have been glad to abolish writing,

15

and go back to the use of quippos ?   Would he
have had neighbouring peoples live all their lives
without any intercourse ?   He was a dreamer,
a "glorious dreamer," if you like, but after all
only a dreamer.

viii. There is but one more point in his system
of thought, to which I wish to draw attention.

Does the Tâo Teh King recognise the existence of God?

Professor Douglas says that "Lâo-tsze knew
nothing of a Personal God, so far as we may
judge from this treatise ; " adding, "And indeed
a belief in such a being would be in opposition
to the whole tenor of his philosophy."[1]   To
me the point is by no means so clear.   The
ancient Chinese, we saw in the first Lecture,
calling the visible sky by the name t'ien, used
the same term to express their concept of a
Supreme Power, under Whose rule they were.[2]
Now, Lâo-tsze does this just in the same way
as Confucius.   "The way of Heaven" occurs
five or six times with no adjunct that would be
strange in the Shû or the Shih.[3]   We read

[1] Confucianism and Tâoism, p. 211.
[2] Pp. 8, 9.
[3] *E.g.*, Chh. 47, 73, 77, 79, 81.

such expressions as "the correlate of Heaven," "Heaven saves," "governing men and serving Heaven."[1]

But when it is said, as in ch. 1, that "Tâo, (conceived of as) having no name, is the beginning of heaven and earth; and (conceived of as) having a name is the mother of all things;" or, as in ch. 6, that "the door of the abyss-mother is the root of heaven and earth," does it not seem that Lâo-tsze made his Tâo prior to Heaven? He certainly makes it prior to heaven and earth, which is a phrase denoting the totality of material existences; but he does not make it prior to Heaven, in the usages of that name of which I have just spoken. "Heaven and earth" seems to be used, we saw, in the Confucian books, as a dualistic name for the one Heaven, but it has not that application in the Tâo Teh King, and because of such predicates of the Tâo as are before us I do not feel called on to admit that Lâo-tsze did not believe in God.

There remains, however, one chapter, which has been understood as showing that "there is no room for a Supreme God in his system."[2] That chapter is the fourth, and says: "Tâo is

[1] Chh. 68, 67, 59.
[2] Confucianism and Tâoism, p. 211.

(like the) emptiness (of a vessel), and the use of it, we may say, must be free from all self-sufficiency. How deep it is, as if it were the author of all things!

"We should make our sharpness blunt, and unravel the complications of things; we should attemper our brightness, and assimilate ourselves to the obscurity caused by dust. How still and clear (is Tâo), a phantasm with the semblance of permanence!

" I do not know whose son it is. It might appear to have been before God."

The term employed here for God is Tî, the personal name for the conception of Heaven as the ruling Power,—a term whose origin, as we saw in the first lecture, was in the prehistoric time. Now, Lâo-tsze does not say that he does not believe in God. On the contrary, he accepts the fact of His existence. The sentence does not intimate any negation. All that can be argued from it is that our author makes God posterior, and so inferior, to his Tâo. But he does not really do so. He does not say that Tâo was before God, but that it might appear to have been so. In no chapter does the nature of Tâo as a method or style of action appear more clearly. It has no positive existence of itself; it is but like the emptiness of a vessel, and the manifestation of it by men requires freedom from self-sufficiency. Whence came it? Whose son is it? He cannot tell; but it was probably the perception of this quality in the processes of nature that gave rise to the ideas of God, and led to the use of the name for heaven as the personal Tî.

Such is the interpretation of this difficult chapter in which, after long musing, my mind has found rest. In harmony with it I reply in the affirmative to the question whether the Tâo Teh King recognizes the existence of God.

16. But while the existence of God is not denied, there is no inculcation of religion in the book. **Lâo-tsze's Tâoism is the exhibition of a way or method of living which men should cultivate as the highest and purest development of their nature.** That the name of the system of thought and of the man should be identified, as they are, with the base religion described in the former part of the lecture, is a mystery at present inexplicable. But Tâoism as a discipline for the mind and life has not been without fruit. There have been many who under its influence have withdrawn entirely from the world, and many more who, unable to do that, have endeavoured to keep themselves, while in the world, from the vortex of its ambitions and

passions, seeking after its three precious things, with the stillness of the soul, the simplicity of motive, and the sympathy with virtue and happiness which it commends.[1]

[1] In a recent and excellent work, "The History of Corea," by the Rev. John Ross (J. and B. Parlane, Paisley), the author says that Tâoism, which divides Chinese attention with Buddhism, is almost unknown in Corea (p. 355) ; and in the same chapter he quotes from a native treatise on religion that they have "the Religion of Reason, whose teaching is summed up in the two words ' Clean ' and ' Empty.' " Mr. Ross thinks that this Tâo is meant for Buddhism ; but the Tâoism of Corea is simply that of the Tâo Teh King, while the Tâoist religion is happily unknown.

NOTES ON · LECTURE III.

NOTE A, p. 161.

In b.c. 140, Tung Chung-shû, one of the ablest scholars of the time, replied to a mandate of the emperor Wû with the following counsels :—" The Ch'un Ch'iû magnifies unity of rule and order to show that such is the constant method of heaven and earth, acknowledged to be right in ancient times and the present. Now-a-days every teacher has his own peculiar ways, and every man his own peculiar reasoning. There are a hundred schools with their various arts, all differing in aim and idea, and your Majesty has no means of pursuing any uniform plan, and your regulations are frequently changed, so that your officers and people do not know which to keep. In your servant's humble opinion, all studies not in the six departments of knowledge and other arts sanctioned by Confucius, should be strictly forbidden, and the future proposal of them interdicted. The depraved and perverse talk which we hear will then cease, your regulations may be made uniform, your laws and statutes will be clearly understood, and the people will know what to follow."— " The Illustrated Explanation of the Sacred Edict," by Liang Yen-nien, 1681, on the 7th precept.

Tung's counsel, directed specially against the Tâoism of the day, did not displease the emperor. He raised him to high office, while yet for many years he threw himself blindly into the arms of the charlatans that swarmed to the court. His eyes at length were opened and he bitterly deplored his folly.

NOTE B, p. 161.

In the China Review for May and June last year, there is an able and interesting notice of a proposal for the "Reformation of Missionary enterprise in China." The plan suggested is that, taking advantage of the official arrangements for the regulation and control of heterodox religions, missionaries should become naturalized Chinese subjects, in which case the author of it thinks that " China would be found quite ready to issue the strictest instructions to all authorities to treat them with the utmost justice and consideration, and to put them on the same footing as all scholars and as other priests."

Since 1842 all missionaries have made "treaty rights" the basis of their operations. These give them liberty to preach and make converts, and secure toleration for their converts, and that they shall not be persecuted simply because they have become Christians. This was agreed to by the Chinese government, of course "by constraint, and not willingly." Errors have been committed occasionally by missionaries in trying to extend the protection of the treaties to men who had deceived them, and whose profession of Christianity was only a mask behind which they hoped to secure other ends ; and consuls and foreign ministers have found enforcing compliance with the tolerating article a troublesome affair. I can conceive that some of them would hail the transference of their missionary countrymen with their Chinese converts to the kind and generous hands of the Chinese government ! But such a reformation of the missionary enterprise is a vain dream. The Chinese government could not be expected to deal with different societies and different individuals in detail, and the representatives of different churches and nationalities will not band themselves together to negotiate as one body. Missionaries are content with their position as it is. They know it, and only wish to make the best of it. To the promoters of the proposed scheme, they will only say, "Let well alone."

NOTE C, p. 163.

I hope that some Sinologist will by-and-by, through his researches, be able to give an account of many of these popes of Tâoism. The following jottings, made in the course of my own reading, are not without interest, but I introduce them here to illustrate the extravagance of the system.

The first of the men was Chang Tâo-ling, born in A.D. 34 at T'ien-mû hill in Cheh-chiang, and said to have been a descendant in the eighth generation of Chang Liang, or the marquis Liû, a friend and helper of the founder of the Han dynasty. Having learned the art of prolonging life, he retired among the hills, refusing to come forth, though repeatedly invited to court by the emperors Chang and Ho (A.D. 76—105). For a long time he wandered about, visiting famous hills, and at last came to the rivulet of "Roseate Clouds" in Hsing-an in the east, and followed it up till it brought him to the cave of the same name,—a grotto with its rocks, fit for an Immortal. There he prepared his pill for three years, while green dragons and white tigers wheeled about above him. Having eaten the pill, though he was then sixty years old, he looked younger than ever. He also got a mysterious volume from which he understood the changes and transformations of spirits, and could drive away and destroy imps and demons. Afterwards he came to the peak of Yun-t'âi in Shû, and thence ascended to heaven, leaving his books, talismans, and charms, his sword and seal to his descendants.

The above details are from Yî's Biographical dictionary of 1793. Many others have been collected by Edkins and Chalmers. The latter says (Article on Tâoism in China Review, 1873) :—" Once he slew a million devils with one stroke of a vermilion pencil ; and on the humble intercession of their six kings, who were not quite dead, he raised them all to life again in the same way, on condition that they should go away to the western countries, and no longer infest China."

Tâo-ling's descendants enjoyed the presidency of Tâoism till A.D. 424, when K'âu Hsiên-chih, a famous member of the body, intrigued with a favourite at the court of the Northern Weî, and got himself appointed as the patriarch with the title of " Heavenly Teacher." Of this K'âu the dictionary tells us that he had met with an immortal called Ch'ăng Kung-hsing, and rambled about with him, eating the medicine of the immortals. He then lived retired in Sung-yang till A.D. 424, when he went to court. One day he told a disciple that he had dreamt the night before that Kung-hsing had called him from the palace of the Immortals on the central mountain, on which he was transformed and could fly. A pure vapour, like a pillar of smoke, issued from his mouth, till he had got half-way up the sky, when it melted away, and his body gradually contracted. People said that in this way he had got rid of his body ; and afterwards he was seen on the hill of Sung, with his body of the colour of silver, bright and shining, so that people knew that he had become an Immortal.

I suppose the presidency continued in the line of this K'âu till A.D. 748, when the emperor Hsüan of the T'ang dynasty, distinguished for a time for his Tâoist proclivities, restored it to the Changs. None of them come prominently before us till A.D. 1015, when the Sung emperor Chăn Tsung, as stated in the text of the lecture, endowed Chang Chăng-Sui for himself and his posterity with the freehold of all their lands about Lung-hû hill, and built for him likewise a hall and temple.

The emperors of the Mongol or Yüan dynasty were favourable to Tâoism. Jenghiz Khan himself, indeed, sent for Ch'iû Ch'ang-chun, a very famous professor of the system, to instruct him in it, in 1220. There is a long and interesting account of Ch'iû's travels to Persia, where Jenghiz was at the time, and of his return to China, with all the interviews and intercourse between them, in Dr. Bretschneider's Notes on Chinese Mediæval Travellers to the West (Shanghaî, 1875), from which we receive a high impression of the man. He belonged, indeed, to the school which professes to "refine the heart," and not the pill. Jenghiz granted a decree, releasing all professors of the Tâo from the payment of taxes. These would only be those belonging to "the order." Jenghiz's visitor, however, was not a Chang.

The pope Chang Tsung-yen was invited by Kublai, the first Yüan emperor, in 1276, after he had completed the reduction of Chiang-nan, to visit him in that province. The emperor received him with distinction, and said, "Formerly I sent Wang Yî-ch'ing to consult your father, who returned to me for answer that in twenty years the empire would be united under one rule. The words of the mysterious Immortal have been fulfilled." He then ordered his visitor to be seated, and feasted him. He gave him also a cap gorgeous with ornaments of jade, and a seamless robe of cloth of gold, styled him "the true man, proficient in the Tâo, whose doings were efficacious, the ideal of harmony," and appointed him teacher of Tâoism in Chiang-nan. Giving him a seal of silver, he told him to produce the seal of jade and the precious sword, which had been transmitted from his ancestor. Looking on these, the emperor said to his ministers in waiting, "I know not how many changes of dynasty there have been, but this sword and this seal have been handed

down from father to son to the present day ; certainly
the spiritual intelligences have guarded them." He then
built a temple to the father of his visitor in the capital,
and ordered him to take up his residence at it, but after a
year Tsung-yen begged leave to return to his hill, where
he died in 1292.

The notice in the Biographies goes on to trace the
history of the Changs through several successions, amid
constantly repeated tokens of the imperial favour.

The present Head of Tâoism was in Shanghâi a few
years ago, when several foreigners had interviews with
him. Dr. Edkins was one of them, and asked him
how long it was since the Chang deified as Yü Tí and
Yü Hwang Shang Tî (p. 169) first received that title.
The answer was—" From the beginning of the universe ! "

NOTE D, p. 208.

In the Fâ Lun King, there is an account of nearly
twenty different appearances of Lâo-tsze, from the earliest
prehistoric time that the Chinese imagination has conceived down to the time of Confucius. It says : " In
the time of king K'ang (B.C. 1078—1053) when he was
known as the philosopher Kwo Shû, he went out by the
pass on the west, and returned across the desert to
instruct Confucius (B.C. 517) on the subject of ceremonies." It then states who were his teachers in heaven
and among men, and adds : " When Lâo-tsze was born, he
jumped up and took nine steps in the air, while lotus
flowers sprang up under his feet. Pointing to heaven
with his right hand and with his left hand to the earth,
he said, ' In heaven above and earth beneath only the
Tâo is honourable.' When Shakyamuni was born, he
jumped up and took seven steps in the air, pointing with
one hand to heaven and with the other to the earth, and

saying, ' In heaven above and earth beneath, only I am honourable.' " The author then naïvely remarks that " the two incidents ought not to have been so much alike ! " Of course they ought not. Neither of them occurred. Both are legends, and that about Lâo-tsze is modelled from the other.

IV.

*THE CHINESE RELIGIONS, AS COM-
PARED WITH CHRISTIANITY.*

黜異端以崇正學

"Discountenance strange principles in order to exalt the correct doctrine."—*K'ang-hsî Edict, 7th Precept.*

"God, who at sundry times and in divers manners spake in time past to the fathers by the prophets, hath in these last days spoken to us by His Son."—*Epistle to the Hebrews,* i. 1, 2.

IV.

Object and method of this lecture.

1. I HAVE endeavoured in three lectures to describe the two indigenous religions of China,—if, indeed, we may say that Tâoism, which, as a religion, has borrowed so much from Buddhism, is indigenous. My object in this concluding lecture will be to treat of both Confucianism and Tâoism as compared with Christianity. I assume, you will perceive, that you are all acquainted with Christianity, and do not need to be instructed by me as to its facts and principles. The name which first occurred to me for the course of four lectures was "Confucianism, Tâoism, and Christianity," but I soon felt that that required modification. It was right that I should teach you what the first two systems are, having spent more than half my life in making myself acquainted with them, and in endeavouring to bring over their adherents to the faith of Christ; but it would not be congruous, nor is it needful for me, to set forth to you in

the same way what Christianity is. Most of
you know your Bibles as well as I do ; and
there are those among you at whose feet it
would be proper for me to sit as a learner
concerning the history and doctrines of our
religion.

I will conduct the argument in this lecture,
therefore, on the assumption that you are acquainted with Christianity ; and I will compare
what you have now learned about the Chinese
religions with what we have all known, more
or less fully, about the other from our early
years. It may be said that my reasoning
will proceed from and conduct to a foregone
conclusic   To some extent it must and will
be so. I c. nnot make my mind a *tabula rasa*
in regard to the faith in which I was brought
up, and which, in mature years, after not a
little speculation and hesitancy, I embraced
for myself, with an entire conviction of its
truth. At the same time, the more that
a man possesses the Christian spirit, and is
governed by Christian principle, the more
anxious will he be to do justice to every other
system of religion, and to hold his own without
taint or fetter of bigotry. Looking abroad
on the various forms of belief in the world,
and including his own among them, he will

endeavour to fulfil the counsel of Paul, to "prove all things and hold fast that which is good."

So far as the Confucian, Tâoist, and Christian systems are concerned, this is what I now wish to do with you. Of course I shall freely state my own views on the various subjects on which I touch. They will not jar much, if at all, on those which you have been accustomed to hold. If some of you should think that my trumpet gives now and then an uncertain sound, or if my sentiments shall seem here too narrow and there too wide, I ask from you the exercise of your charity. The field of Christian truth is very large. There is space in it for agreement of opinion; and round every doctrine there is a margin where allowance can be made for differences of conception and statement. I think we are of one mind in this. In this special application of his words, we say with Horace,

"*Scimus, et hanc veniam petimusque damusque vicissim.*"

I will proceed therefore to compare, it may be to contrast, various points in Confucianism and Tâoism, but especially in Confucianism, with the teaching of Christianity on the same subjects. Having done this, I will direct attention to

Christian doctrines that are peculiar, and consider whether the study of the religions of China should make us thankful for such doctrines or the contrary. I will not plunge, however, into the sea of theology or Christology, but be guided, as to the topics which I take up, by the study which I have pursued with you of the two Chinese systems. I may be allowed in conclusion to insist on two practical issues to which our discussions should lead.

Preliminary points of agreement in the three religions.

2. Before entering on the comparison or contrast which I propose, there are three things in which the religions agree, that are very important, and which it is desirable to specify.

i. There is **the existence of God.** The first verse of our Bible declares this :—" In the beginning God created the heaven and the earth." We discovered the divine name as familiar to the Chinese in the earliest of their historical documents. We were able even to satisfy ourselves that that name was familiar to them at a period long anterior to any of their written books. Neither in our Bible nor in the books of Confucianism is an attempt made to prove the divine existence. In the book of Isaiah Jehovah says, " I am Jehovah, and there is none else. There is no God beside me." The Confucian books do not contain a similar declaration ; but we saw how the monotheism of prehistoric time in China has always striven, and not without success, to assert itself against attempts to corrupt it. In Tâoism, which is polytheistic, the name of God is of course common ; but Lâo-tsze himself often spoke of God, so far as the term T'ien', " Heaven," employed in a non-material sense, could do so, and on one occasion he used the name God itself. The existence of God is assumed in the three religions.

ii. The idea of the possibility and the fact of revelation is also common to them all. We are familiar with the opening words of the epistle to the Hebrews :—" God, who at sundry times and in divers manners spake in time past unto the fathers by the prophets, hath in these last days spoken to us by His Son." Among the primitive written characters of the Chinese there was one, we saw, which was the symbol of manifestation or revelation coming from above. That God should speak or make known His will to men did not seem strange to the Chinese fathers, and in the Shih we read that "God spake to king Wăn," just as we read in the Old Testament that "God spake to Moses." Hundreds of Tâoist tracts also are circulated in China, each one purporting to be the teaching of this god or that, "to warn," or "to advise mankind." The idea of revelation therefore is held in the three religions.

iii. And so is the idea of **the supernatural.** I do not know that I am able, and certainly I will not attempt, to talk learnedly or philosophically of supernaturalism. We have to do here with the simplest conception of it,—the occurrence of events in which we recognise the immediate presence and operation of God. I spoke in the first lecture of the view of Confucius about the ever-changing phenomena of the material universe.[1] He thought they were produced by the mysterious spiritual operation of God. Such a theory may be right or wrong. If it mean more than that the phenomena occur in accordance with and by means of general laws established by God and within the range of His omniscience, it seems to be needless and only to cumber us in our study of nature. But events so happening are not supernatural. When, however, we read in the Shîh King that the mother of Hâu-chî happened to

[1] Pp. 42, 43.

tread on a toe-print made by God, and in consequence became pregnant, and in due time gave birth to her wonderful son,[1] we have passed from the region of the natural into that of the supernatural.

But so many of the things regarded and related as supernatural have, upon careful investigation of them, been demonstrated to be the delusions of error and superstition, or the fabrications of deceit, having nothing about them, if they really occurred, which did not admit of natural interpretation, that we are often inclined to reject the idea of the supernatural altogether. On the other hand, when we have admitted the fact of the divine existence, and of the interest that God retains in all His handiworks as the product of His power, and especially in men as the most intelligent of His creatures and the special objects of His love;—when we have admitted these things, we dare not deny the possibility of God's supernatural, or rather extraordinary, interference both in nature and in providence. When any such interference is asserted, we dare not disbelieve without examination. Did it take place or not? The conclusion of our judgment allows its possibility ; the yearning of our hearts suggests its probability. The

[1] Shih, III. ii., Ode 1.

question comes to be one of evidence, and we are not without sufficient tests of truth to guide us to a conclusion in which we feel assured our minds will be able to repose. At any rate, Christianity, Confucianism, and Tâoism, all allow the element of the supernatural, all assert the fact of revelation, all acknowledge the existence of God. On each of these points there are great differences in the three religions when we go into detail; but the things themselves are admitted by them all.

Comparison as to the doctrine and worship of God.

3. The first lecture on Confucianism was devoted to its doctrine and worship of God. We were glad to find in the Shû and Shîh so much about God and His government of men which we could without hesitation accept as true. At the same time, whatever of this kind is to be found in these and the other classical books exists only in shreds and patches. The contrast between them and the overflowing fulness of the Old and New Testaments on the same theme is remarkable. Our sacred writers excel themselves when they dilate on God. Very often what we read in them professes to be the word of God about Himself coming to us by them. In no

other volume does human genius soar so grandly in its attempts to rise to the height of its great argument. Chapters in Job, many of the Psalms, the fortieth chapter of Isaiah, and many other portions of prophecy, cause us to be still, and know that God has brought Himself nigh, and is speaking to us by and through His servants. We can only bow our heads and worship. Nature and providence also seem to become alive in the Bible, and add their voices to the testimony concerning God :—"The heavens declare His glory ; the firmament showeth His handiwork. Day unto day uttereth speech ; night unto night showeth knowledge." The declarations and doxologies of the New Testament, briefer than those of the Old, have yet a depth and force peculiar and unrivalled. Take for instance those two short sentences in the first epistle of John,—" God is light," and " God is love." You will search in vain all the Confucian literature of China for anything approaching to them.

But as you saw, for the fullest expression of the Confucian doctrine of God, we must have recourse not to the classical writings, but to the ,solstitial prayers. They are to be found in the rituals and statutes of the empire generally ; but these are not intended for popular reading.

And the prayers occupy but a small portion of those great collections, and, if not specially sought for, are likely to be overlooked. Here and there a scholar may have made himself acquainted with them, but to the masses of the people they are as if they were not. They have not been taught them at school, and it is improbable that their attention was called to them after they left it. How different it is with the doctrine of God as delivered in the Bible! That doctrine is the chief thing in it. We cannot read many pages of it thoughtfully without receiving more or less of it into our minds. And our sacred scriptures appeal to us, claiming to be read and studied. The possession of them is our greatest privilege. The young man is told that he should cleanse his way by taking heed to it according to them. They are intended to be to every man his delight and counsellors ; a lamp to his feet and a light to his path. " Search the scriptures " is an injunction that resounds through both the Testaments. As the Christian doctrine of God is fuller and more exalted than the Confucian, so the provision made for men's becoming acquainted with it in the different character of the books of the two religions is incomparably greater.

I go on to speak of the worship of God in them. Here Confucianism is very defective. The formal organized worship is restricted to the emperor. The occasions for it are few, and of the people there are none with him. It is indeed a wonderful fact to think of, that a worship of the one God has been maintained in the vicinity of their capitals by the sovereigns of China almost continuously for more than four thousand years. I felt this fact profoundly when I stood early one morning by the altar of Heaven, in the southern suburb of Peking. It was without my shoes that I went up to the top of it; and there around the central slab of the marble with which it was paved, free of flaw as the cœrulean vault above, hand in hand with the friends who accompanied me, I joined in singing the doxology, beginning—

"Praise God from whom all blessings flow."

I rejoice in the imperial worship of God, but I can never sufficiently regret that this shaped itself even in prehistoric time into a representative worship by the Head of the state, instead of being extended throughout the nation, and joined in by the multitudes of the people. They know that the worship is performed, but they have not seen it, nor taken part in it. There is for them only in general the inarticulate reverence of Heaven, with groans and appeals to It, or to God in heaven, when they are suffering under oppression or other calamity. I have seen "the upward glancing of the eye" to the sky above, and "the falling of the tear" in the bitterness of grief, and I have seen them with satisfaction and thankfulness. But what a pity that the Chinese were not taught from the first to draw nigh to God, in all the changes of their lot, as their King, their Shepherd, and their Friend!

The worship of God in ancient Israel was a truly national worship. From all parts of the country the people went up on their great occasions to the place where God had recorded His name to offer their sacrifices, perform their vows, and present their supplications. When Solomon inaugurated the services of the temple, "he stood before the altar of the Lord in the presence of all the congregation of Israel, and spread forth his hands towards heaven." "Hearken Thou," he said, "to the supplication of Thy servant, and of Thy people Israel, when they shall pray towards this place." Solomon's petitions went up also for other men, who were not of the people Israel,—for the stranger who

should come and pray towards the temple.
"Hear Thou," he said, "in heaven Thy
dwelling-place, and do according to all that
the stranger calleth to Thee for, that all people
of the earth may know Thy name to fear Thee
as do Thy people Israel." From the first it
was intimated that the house of God in
Jerusalem should be "called an house of prayer
for all people."

This intention regarding the worship of God
in Israel began to be fully realized after the
institution of the Christian Church. The time
then came when not alone in Jerusalem, or in
any other locality, should men worship God.
A true spirit of devotion converts every spot
into an altar whence prayer and praise may
arise to heaven. Wherever men seek Him,
God is found. The way of approach to Him
is open to individuals, to families, to great
congregations. The worshipping sovereign will
pray for his people; the worshipping people
will pray for their sovereign. Add to this the
liberty of worship which Christianity proclaims
to all, and its various solemnities ;—the setting
apart one day in seven specially for them,
the reading of the Scriptures, the hymns
of praise, the exercises of prayer, the word of
instruction and exhortation :—before all this

the worship of God in Confucianism fades away into a small and imperfect thing.

Once again, on this topic. The worship of God in Confucianism is vitiated by an inferior worship paid to a multitude of spirits, either by the emperor in person, or by some minister commissioned by him. It is true that this does not amount to polytheism, for those spirits do not receive the divine name, are not called gods. It is true also that the functions ascribed to them arise from offices with which they are supposed to be intrusted by God for the promotion of the welfare of men. And as we saw from the prayer addressed to them by an emperor of the Ming dynasty to which I drew your special attention in the first lecture,[1] they act as intercessors with God on behalf of His worshippers. But the thought that such intercession is necessary tends to separate between men and God, making them think of Him as severe and dwelling in too great state to be approached by them directly. The supposition, moreover, that such spirits have the government of parts of the world and the care of human affairs committed to them, prevents the Chinese from rising to the full conception of the divine

[1] Pp. 44—46.

omniscience, omnipotence, and omnipresence, I always found it so in my intercourse with the people. They would say that God must have His ministers in different places, carrying on His administration in the spiritual sphere, just as the officers of the emperor were distributed throughout the nation. Much more is this apparent in the Tâoists' account of providence, where the spirit of the furnace and the three spirits of the person repair every month to the court of Heaven, and give in their report of the individuals under their surveillance.

Now the Christian worship of God is free from this depraving admixture of the worship of inferior spirits. It is so certainly in Protestant churches. Spiritual beings, angels, come before us in both the Old Testament and the New. We have "the ministry of angels" in connexion with the giving of the law by Moses; we have the same in connexion with the leading many sons to glory by the Captain of our salvation. But while enough is told us to encourage trust in God, there is nothing to gratify a prurient curiosity, and nothing to make us have recourse to angels as mediators between us and God, or pay any kind of worship, however inferior, to them. In this respect, as in the former, the worship of God

as taught by the Christian church is superior
to that practised in Confucianism.

Comparison as regards filial piety and the worship of ancestors.

4. I proceed now to compare Confucianism
and Christianity in regard to their views on
filial piety and the worship of ancestors. It is
a standing charge, based of course on ignorance
and prejudice, with the Chinese people against
our religion that it is contrary to filial piety.
A name of reproach given to a convert is—
"Unfilial renegade." I have heard a hundred
fierce controversies on the subject closed by
the Confucianist's triumphant appeal, as he
considered it, to the fact that Christians do
not worship their fathers and ancestors. And
I have heard missionaries as unjustly and
provokingly taunt their Chinese hearers with
the charge that their filial duty did not begin
to show itself till after their parents were
dead.

The filial piety taught by Confucius, as I
described it in the second lecture, contains
much that commands our warm approval.
The sage again and again, in his conversations
with his disciples, protested against the view
that the requirements of the duty were satis-

fied, when a sufficient material support was given to the parents. He did so, I believe, in order to correct a tendency in men's minds to think that they had done all that was required of them for their parents when they had ministered that support; and I believe further that the same error was in the mind of the Chinese fathers when they fashioned the character which represents the word h s i â o, or filial piety. I pointed out the peculiarity of its structure,—"an old man seated on, or supported by, his son." The idea of the duty in China from the very first subjected the son too much to his father. Confucius felt this, and many of his utterances on the subject were designed to exalt the conception of the virtue. He would have approved of the language in which it is enjoined in our fifth commandment: "Honour thy father and thy mother." It is hardly necessary for me to say that that h o n o u r involved the idea of support, as was finely declared by Paul, when he wrote, "Honour widows that are widows indeed. But if any widow have children or nephews, let them learn first to show piety at home, and to requite their parents; for that is good and acceptable before God." Both Confucianism and Chrisltianity enjoin filial piety. The fundamenta

17

conception of it in the former system is a ministration of support ; in the latter, a rendering of honour. The Christian conception is the higher of the two.

There is another saying of the apostle Paul that throws light on the different views in regard to filial piety in the two religions. He wrote to the Corinthians—"The children ought not to lay up for the parents, but the parents for the children." I never quoted these words in a circle of Chinese friends without their encountering a storm of opposition. When I tried to show that the sentiment was favourable to the progress of society, and would enable each generation to start from a higher standpoint, I found it difficult to obtain a hearing. Even in a matter like this the different tendencies of the Chinese and Christian races manifest themselves. The third chapter of the Bible sounds a note of hope to be realized in the future. Confucian literature only directs its readers to the past. " Onwards and upwards," is the motto on the Christian banner. The Chinese banner in the Confucian camp bears on it, "Back to the times of the early sages ; " that in the Tâoist camp says, "Back to the early Arcadian simplicity."

Christianity knows nothing of the outcome

of filial duty which appears in the Confucian worship of parents and of ancestors generally. It accepts with silent sorrow the fact that they have gone from the circle in which they moved on earth. The thought that God has taken them away intensifies the worship of Him and the prayer to be enabled reverently to submit to His will .and doing ; but as to the departed, there remains only the remembrance of them treasured in the loving heart. Their bodies cannot be brought back, nor their spirits. It is vain to try to have communion with them over any religious feast, though the recollection of them will often be most vivid in the hours of intensest religious exercise. But Christianity has no worship of the dead, and its belief and practice in reference to them are more healthy and true than those of Confucianism. I cannot but think, indeed, that Confucius himself stood in doubt about the worship of the dead which he inherited as an ancient institution of his people. He was not sure about it ; he strove to be sincere in his own observance of it; but he had no complacency in it, and repressed the curious questions which it naturally awakened in the minds of his more thoughtful disciples.

The religion of Tâoism takes an attitude to

the dead very different from that of Confucianism. It believes about them it knows
not what. It requires a vast expenditure from
their surviving friends to secure rest for them
in their graves, and to deliver them from the
courts of the horrible purgatory through which
they have to pass. Of course Christianity is as
much opposed to all this as it is to the Confucian
worship of the dead. That worship also is a
superstition, only not so repelling as the horrors
which Tâoism " imagines howling." Inculcating
filial piety in its highest and widest legitimate
meaning, Christianity keeps itself clear of all
the abuses connected with it in the Chinese
religions.

Comparison as regards the teaching of morality.

5. At this point I take up the consideration
of the merits of the three religions as regards
the morality which they inculcate. It might
seem more natural to treat here of what they
teach about a future state, as belonging to
the sphere of religion or the exhibition of
our relations with the invisible ; but I wish first
to compare their moral teaching, because the
subject of a future state will lead me away, for

a time at least, from the Chinese systems to what is peculiar to Christianity.

Its inculcation of human duty has been regarded as the glorious distinction of Confucianism from the time that the Roman Catholic missionaries made the Chinese sage and his lessons known in Europe. Pope gave him his place in the temple of fame because of the way in which he "taught men to be good." And there is much that is admirable in the Chinese view of the constitution of human society, and the duties belonging to its several relationships. Far be it from me to say a word or insinuate a thought against it! I have been forward for many years to profess my agreement with its doctrine of human nature as being formed for goodness; for, if it were not so, I do not see how man could be exhorted, under any system of religion, "to eschew evil and do good." Confucius believed that he had a mission from Heaven in connexion with the cause of truth, and there is no reason why we should hesitate to accept the belief. He for the most part well fulfilled the trust. He unfolded the moral teachings of the earlier sages, bringing out the spirit of them while he maintained the letter; requiring an inward sincerity in all outward practice, and pouring scorn on the pharisaism which contents itself with the cleansing of the outside of the cup and platter. Even though we are obliged to admit his own great deficiencies in the " Spring and Autumn " annals, we need not shrink from allowing that he was a messenger from God to his countrymen for good, for it never was the way of God to reveal all truth at once by His chosen instruments, or to make them by their calling infallible, so that they should not err in judgment or stumble in practice.

Certainly Confucius discharged his duty as a guardian of morality when he delivered the golden rule, even in the negative form in which he always gave it. His countrymen are as familiar with it as we are with the form in which it is presented in the Sermon on the Mount; and from other lessons that he left them, they understand it not only as a negative, but also as a positive rule.

If we turn now to Lâo-tsze, while we do not find the golden rule in the Tâo Teh King, we have there noble exhibitions of the virtue of humility, of the casting out from the breast every taint of selfish motive, and of the power of meekness to overcome evil; all culminating in the precept, which even Confucius could not receive, to return good for evil. The morality of Tâoism, as now taught in millions of copies of the " Book of Actions and their Retributions," while not unaffected by the grotesque characteristics and superstitions of the religion, still bears on it the stamp of the "venerable philosopher." All honour to him and his contemporary!

But we have the precepts that give glory to the two men from the lips of the one Christ. He said, "All things whatsoever ye would that men should do unto you, do ye even so to them." He said also, and in the same discourse, "Love your enemies, bless them that curse you, do good to them that hate you, and pray for them that despitefully use you and persecute you." I do not say, "Take his crown from Confucius, take his crown from Lâo-tsze, and give them both to Christ." On His head are many crowns, and this one among them,—the crown of the best and noblest teacher of morality.

It has been said, indeed, that Confucius' rule and also Lâo-tsze's precept were given in the sixth century before our era; but Christ subjoined to his version of the rule that to the same effect was the teaching of "the law and the prophets," and we may consider it as but another form of the injunction, "Thou shalt love thy neighbour as thyself," which was as old as Moses. Nor was the teaching of the great issue of the tâo in our Bible less ancient; we

read in the book of Proverbs, "If thine enemy
be hungry, give him bread to eat; and if he be
thirsty, give him water to drink." I refer thus
to the antiquity of the sentiments in our Scriptures simply as a matter of fact, and not from
any wish to detract from the merit of the
Chinese philosophers in giving expression to
them. That we find their definite enunciation
of them, shows to what a height in moral
science human nature is capable of attaining;
it shows how deeply God has written the work
of His law in the hearts of men, and fitted
them thereby to be a law to themselves.

And it is with no unkindly feeling that I
call attention, in connexion with this topic of
morality, to Confucius' confession that he was
unable to take the initiative in carrying out his
own rule,[1] and to the fact that Lâo-tsze gave
up the struggle with the evil of his times,
and withdrew into obscurity.[2] The sage's
acknowledgment of his moral feebleness, and
the philosopher's hiding himself from the
evils that he could not remedy, do not lessen
our regard for them and our appreciation of
their worth; but nothing of the kind can be
referred to in the history of Christ. "He did
no sin, neither was guile found in His mouth;

[1] Page 138.   [2] Page 207.

when He was reviled He reviled not again ; when He suffered He threatened not. He went about doing good, leaving an example that we should walk in His steps. He worked while it was day, nor ceased till the night came when no man can work." He was both a perfect teacher and a perfect exemplar of what He taught. K'ung and Lî were good men, but the thought never arises of their being anything more than men. Before Christ, on the other hand, we feel that we are in the presence of one whose participation of our human nature we do not doubt, while we are often ready to exclaim, " Never man spake or did as He ! "

Place of woman in the three religions.

I shall not find a better place than this, at the close of what I have to say on their teaching of morality, to speak of the different places in the social scale given by the three religions to woman. No special mention is made of her in the Tâo Teh King; but I quoted in the last lecture, when treating of the Tâoist purgatory, a brief but emphatic sentence from the " Divine Panorama," which speaks volumes as to the estimate formed of her. A woman who escapes some of the tortures of purgatory in consequence of her virtuous deeds, and is allowed to return to life and the world for another period of probation, " shall be born," it is said, " as a man." The sentiment and even the words are of Buddhistic origin, but Tâoism has made them its own. In Confucianism the position of woman has always been an inferior one, and I will not repeat the illustrations which were given of it in the second lecture. It is only Christianity that vindicates for woman a position of equality with man. As in the Christian church, in respect of privilege, there is no distinction of nation or race or rank, so also there is none of sex. " In Christ Jesus there is neither male nor female." His religion, indeed, still leaves the husband the head of the family, as he is to fight the battle of life in society and be the bread-winner ; but even the feebler frame of the wife, which renders this subordination necessary, is turned in the New Testament to her advantage. How fine is the language of Peter, "Ye husbands, dwell with them according to knowledge, giving honour to the wife, as to the weaker vessel, and as being heirs together of the grace of life, that your prayers be not hindered"! And still finer, perhaps, is the language of Paul. Having required that wives be subject in all things to their husbands, as the church is subject to Christ, he adds, " Husbands, love your wives, even as Christ also loved the church, and gave Himself for it, that He might sanctify and cleanse it, that He might present it to Himself a glorious church, not having spot or wrinkle or any such thing ; but that it should be holy and without blemish."

The account of the formation of Eve, and the union of her and Adam, given in the second chapter of Genesis, is expressive and instructive. It follows from it that monogamy was intended to be the rule of human marriage. It came to pass that this ordinance was set aside at a very early time, and divorce and polygamy were permitted even in the Jewish state, though its prophets were commissioned to testify that Jehovah had made but one wife for one man at the first, and that " He hated putting away." Still the evil continued, but it was not permitted to pass into the Christian church. As He did not in regard to any other social institution, Christ took in regard to marriage the position of a legislator, and insisted that the original intention should be enforced. Only by one act of guilt on the part of the wife, in itself a repudiation of the marriage bond, could divorce be made possible.

Apart from that, what God had joined man must not put asunder. When Christian churches began to be formed in different places, Paul proclaimed the law of Christ concerning marriage, that "every man have his own wife, and every woman her own husband." In China again, the wife enters into the patriarchal system of her husband's family virtually a servant to his mother, whereas Christ in this respect also proclaimed the original rule, "A man shall leave father and mother, and shall cleave to his wife."

I need not dwell longer on this topic. It is only by Christianity that woman has accorded to her a place of equality by the side of her husband, his honoured and cherished companion, and the one mistress of his household. It is only, moreover, under Christianity that she can move with freedom in society, and exert her legitimate influence in favour of all that is good and beautiful and pure. In every department of morality, in a word, our religion is superior to the religions of China.

Comparison as regards the teaching about a future state.

6. There is but one more of the subjects dwelt upon in my former lectures on which

I have to compare the other two religions with Christianity; and it will be found that the result is as favourable to it in this as in the other cases. The subject is their teaching about a future state.

The old religion of China says very little about this. The primitive term for spirit,[1] and that for the manes of the deceased,[2] tell how the fathers believed that man consisted of body and soul, and that, when he died and the body mingled with the dust, the soul continued to live on. Passages in the classical books say further that the soul ascends on high. One ancient sovereign, a man of heroic virtue and sagely wisdom, is spoken of in the Shû as being in heaven, and attended there by the spirits of the ministers who had served him on earth, while both he and they took an interest in what was happening in the kingdom that they had left.[3] Another sovereign, whose earthly career had been marked by every excellent quality, is represented in the Shih as ascending and descending on the left and right of God in heaven.[4] These are special cases, and I cannot call to mind any general statements in the Confucian classics as to the state of the dead.

[1] Pp. 11, 12.   [2] P. 13.
[3] Pp. 113, 114.   [4] The Shih, iii. i., Ode 1.

The ancient belief of the continued existence of the soul or spirit found its expression, even in prehistoric time, in the worship of parents and ancestors, taking, we saw, the form of a feast as the symbol of a family reunion. When Confucius appeared and devoted his life mainly to the study of antiquity, and inculcating the lessons which he thus learned on his disciples, he added nothing to these scanty hints about futurity. Connecting the worship of the dead with filial piety, he derived additional motives with which to enforce the cultivation of that virtue. At the same time he rather evaded the questions that were put to him about the state of the dead, and avoided, as much as he could, speaking at all on the subject. The truth is, he could not tell what he did not know, he could not instruct others in what he had not learned for himself. I do not blame him for his silence. But the Chinese are left by the Confucian religion with a very limited and uncertain knowledge of futurity, with merely a hint or two that the souls of their departed friends are in heaven ; with no account of what sort of a place or state heaven is ; with no intimation of a discriminating retribution for the good and evil of the life on earth in the life beyond.

No doubt the barrenness of their religion in

this respect disposed the Chinese to give heed to the teachings of Buddhism about transmigration, and to fall victims to the cruel representations of Tâoism in its courts of purgatory and the horrors of hell. We cannot tell how Tâoism got its trichotomy of the human spirit, with one soul cleaving to the tablet of wood, another haunting the grave, and the third hungry and naked, a starved and homeless ghost shivering somewhere in the air, or tortured in purgatory; but the care of their dead thus multiplied is too great a burden for the living to bear. And it is little comfort they receive from the hope that their friends may have got to be Immortals of heaven with three thousand good deeds at their credit, or even Immortals of earth at the low price of three hundred. All in Tâoism about futurity is too fantastic or too horrible to be of use for comfort to the intelligent mind in distress, or for encouragement and guidance in the pursuit of virtue.

When we turn to the New Testament, we read in it that " Jesus Christ abolished death, and brought life and immortality to light through the gospel." The temple of Christ's own body is destroyed, and in three days He raises it up again. While put to death in the flesh, in the activity of His spiritual nature, He goes and preaches to the spirits in prison. The parable of the rich man and Lazarus shows that, immediately on death, there is a separation of the good and the bad; that each class goes to its own place, and that retribution commences according to the character of the life. Christ also proclaimed that "the time is coming when all that are in their graves shall hear His voice and come forth : they that have done good to the resurrection of life, and they that have done evil to the resurrection of condemnation."

Christianity thus teaches that there is a future life for man; that the consciousness of the spirit is not interrupted by the event of death; and that, according to the character of the life that has been lived, there is an immediate experience of good or evil in the invisible world ; that a time is coming in the future when there will be a resurrection of the dead, to be followed by a public and general judgment; that "the Lord will bring to light the hidden things of darkness, and make manifest the counsels of the hearts ; " and finally, that every true servant of Christ shall then have his proper meed of praise, and every other who, weighed in the balance of the divine judgment, has been found wanting shall receive according to the ill desert of his deeds.

Peculiarities in the disclosures of the future by Christianity.

7. Such are the teachings of Christianity. I will not adduce many texts in proof and illustration of the points which I have indicated. The time is not sufficient for me to do so ; and I said at the outset that you were all acquainted with the sacred books of our religion. But in the presence of these things about the future which are most surely believed among us, we feel that there ceases to be comparison any longer between the religions of China and Christendom. Confucianism has next to nothing to show about futurity. Tâoism would still less deserve our regard in this respect but for the lurid light in which it has placed its courts of purgatory and an everlasting hell. Without stopping to touch here on this recent development of it, I wish at this stage in the lecture to point out two things.

The positive element in the Christian representation of future blessedness.

The former of them is the one positive element in which the New Testament sums up the blessedness of his future being to him who has died in the faith of Christ ;—it is the "being with Christ." How shall a positive idea of heaven be conveyed to us ? Paul tells us that "he knew a man in Christ, who was caught up (whether in the body or out of the body he could not tell)—caught up into paradise." Surely that man told him much about the glories of the blessed state. No ; what he heard there were "unspeakable words, which it is not lawful for a man to utter." We are all aware how the figures of earthly things are employed to give us an idea of heaven by being divested of the temporal and changing character that belongs to them here. When heaven is called, for instance, "an inheritance," it is one that is "incorruptible, undefiled, and that fadeth not away." An endeavour is made to give us, by means of those negations, some conception of the better world. But here is this one positive idea of "being with Christ." Christ Himself took the lead in putting this forward. He said to His disciples, "In my Father's house are many mansions ; I go to prepare a place for you. And if I go and prepare a place for you, I will come again and receive you to myself, that, where I am, there ye may be also." On the cross He said to the penitent by His side, "To-day shalt thou be with me in paradise." "Absent from the body, present with the Lord," is the apostle Paul's description of the future ; and he tells the Philippians that, if it lay only with himself, he would die at once rather than live, for to die would be "to depart and be with Christ, which was far better." Similarly, after the resurrection and the judgment, "we shall be ever with the Lord." This great element of the heavenly bliss is most important. It is apprehensible by all. People's thoughts about heaven will differ according to the varieties of their earthly experience and attainments ; but as the hearts of all His disciples burned within them when they communed with Jesus on earth, so all cán understand how sweet it will be to have unending companionship with Him, and to be guided and led by Him to all which infinity and eternity have to show and to give. May I be allowed to illustrate the subject here by the case of a Chinese female convert? She had been "a wise woman," a professor among her countrywomen of Tâoist superstitions. I forget how she was brought to the faith of Christ, but I remember clearly her earnest, useful life as a member of the church. Her previous occupation had sharpened her faculties. Of her own accord she went about among her neighbours telling them of the gospel. She was taken ill, and I visited her repeatedly at the house of the married daughter with whom she lived, and was refreshed by her conversation. When I went in one forenoon, the daughter was seated on a stool with her mother in her lap, and was putting on her her best clothes. " She is unconscious," she said, looking up at me ; " and while her limbs are yet supple, I am putting on her her best clothes, that she may be in readiness for the coffin." While I was saying something in reply, my voice fell on the ear of the dying woman. She opened her eyes, turned her face to me, and tried to speak, but could only give vent to a low, indistinct murmur. " Death is near at hand," I said ; " but is your faith firm in Jesus ? Do you feel that, departing, you will be with Him ? " A light of intelligence irradiated her sunken features. Again she tried in vain to speak. Turning her eyes upwards, and raising her forefinger, she pointed towards heaven ; and while she was in this attitude, the spirit passed away. You will not wonder that my eyes were suffused with tears, and that, as I left the house, I was thinking of the death of Stephen, when he, looking up steadfastly to heaven, said, " Behold, I see the heavens opened, and the Son of man standing at the right hand of God."

The Christian revelation of futurity rests on the resurrection of Christ.

The second thing which I wish to point out here, in connexion with the disclosures of the future by Christianity, is, that they all rest on the event of our Lord's resurrection, which the New Testament writers assert in the most direct and positive terms. The supernatural element in our religion here comes out prominently; and if the record in our books concerning it be admitted as true, a most important distinction between Christianity on the one hand and Confucianism and Tâoism on the other is established. THEY are of men and by man,—not without God indeed, but with Him only as all things are included in the circle of His knowledge and ordination; IT is of God, and by God, specially revealed to make known the path of duty and the way of life.

Results of the comparison thus far, and further pursuit of the subject.

8. The results of the comparison thus far conducted have all been favourable to Chris-

tianity.   Confucianism is both more ancient and of a higher type than Tâoism ; but Christianity far transcends Confucianism in all the points which we have considered.   What is good in Confucianism appears more full and complete in it ; what is wrong in Confucianism is corrected in it ; what is defective in Confucianism is supplied in it.   And now the train of my reasoning has brought us face to face with the questions :—Is the difference between Christianity and the religions of China in kind and not merely in degree ?   Is it THE religion while each of them is merely A religion ?

We shall have made an important step towards answering these questions in the affirmative, if we accept the resurrection of Christ, related in the New Testament, as having actually taken place.   And I for one do not hesitate to do so.   Some one will say that the resurrection would have been a supernatural event ; but as no supernatural event is possible, therefore the record of it must be rejected as false.   But I cannot grant the postulate that no supernatural event is possible. God is the author, upholder, and arranger of nature.   The antecedents and consequents in its phenomena occur in the order which He prescribes, and according to laws which He has ordained. But when He had finished "the heavens and the earth and all the host of them,"—when He had given existence to the various tribes of living things "with," as the Chinese say, "their reproducing power,"—He did not withdraw, if I may venture so to speak, into the solitude of His own being, and make a law for Himself never to reappear, and never to interfere, whatever disorders might arise, whatever danger there might seem to be of His purposes in creation being frustrated. God is and must be free to act, according to His wisdom and the resources of His nature, when and how it seems good to Him. Action on the part of God is what I call the supernatural. No argument of metaphysical reasoning and no inference from the facts of physical philosophy have ever shaken for a moment my belief in the possibility of the supernatural or miraculous.

Confucianism and Tâoism, as we saw, do not deny the supernatural. There is no dispute between them and Christianity as to miracles. Tâoism, indeed, runs riot in its multitude of them, grotesque, unsubstantiated, aimless. They are ridiculed by the Confucianists, as in the passage which I quoted in the second Lecture from Wang Yû-po's paraphrase of the amplifi-

cation of the K'ang-hsî edict. But Confucianism itself asserts supernatural events. When
we cast out the marvellous legends that grew
up round the life of the sage, there are still
certain statements by him concerning the
formation of the diagrams of Fû-hsî, and the
use of the Yî King in divination, which bear
the stamp of the supernatural,—a supernatural
that we are constrained to reject just as we
reject the "strange stories" of Tâoism.[1] But
neither religion, as I said, will quarrel with
Christianity for allowing the possibility and
even the occurrence of supernatural events.
Indeed, the primitive character shih, to which
I called attention in the first Lecture as the
symbol of revelation or manifestation from
above,[2] carried the belief of such possibility
from the minds of the prehistoric fathers into
those of their posterity through all time.

The evidence of the resurrection of Christ.

9. We are free therefore, so far as the reason
of the thing and the religions with which I am
comparing Christianity are concerned,—we are
free to consider whether the evidence of the

[1] See the Great Appendix to the Yî, Pt. i. p. 73.
[2] Pp. 12, 13.

resurrection of Christ is satisfactory. I cannot of course attempt anything approaching to a complete exhibition of that evidence. It must suffice to indicate the considerations on which my own mind rests in believing that the event took place.

i. Christ, while He was yet alive, expected and foretold both His death and resurrection. At a certain period in His history, He "began to show to His disciples how that He must go to Jerusalem and be killed, and be raised again the third day." He said, "I have power to lay my life down, and I have power to take it again." It was well known in Judea, to His enemies as well as His friends, that Christ had spoken such things, and that He expected and intended to rise again after He was put to death, for when the chief priests and Pharisees went to Pilate to ask that the sepulchre should be made sure, the ground of their application was, "We remember, that that deceiver said, while he was yet alive, 'After three days I will rise again.'"

That Christ was Himself deluded in the expectation that He would rise again, or that He meant to deceive others about the matter, is to me equally inconceivable. And yet on the assumption that the supernatural is impossible,

He expected what could not be, and said that He would bring the impossibility to pass ! Could this be in the case of Him, the greatest of moral teachers in the long line of all the ages, and " Who did no sin " ?   If it were so, we should have in Him an inexplicable phenomenon.   If His word failed,

> " The pillared firmament is rottenness,
> And earth's base built on stubble."

Because Christ said that He would rise again, I cannot doubt that He did do so.

ii. The fact of the resurrection is confirmed to us by abundant evidence.   Never was an event testified to by witnesses more entitled to credit from their general character, or who had better opportunities of knowing what they related, or who persevered more firmly in their testimony, notwithstanding the disadvantages and even the risk of death to which it exposed them.

iii. I cannot understand how, if the resurrection were not a fact, the story of it came to be palmed successfully on the Christian church. I have never read an attempt to account for this which seemed to me worthy of a refutation.

When an objector therefore asserts that the resurrection of Christ was a physical impossibility, and that the record of it is not to be believed, I reply that the declaration of Christ that it would take place, and the testimony of many that to their personal knowledge it did take place, and the cordial acquiescence of the church in their witness, are three moral impossibilities, if our Lord did not indeed rise from the dead. I place my three moral impossibilities against his one physical impossibility. I myself acknowledge no such physical impossibility. The objector errs in asserting it, not knowing the power of God. At any rate, I believe, and you all, I think, believe with me, that Christ "both died, and rose and revived." The fact of His resurrection accounts for the disclosure of the future state of the Christian believer as a being with Christ, and places Christianity as a religion in a different category from the religions of China.

The Christian scriptures claim to contain a divine revelation.

10. Our acceptance of the record in the New Testament concerning the resurrection of Christ will not satisfy all the demands of Christianity as to the peculiar character of its sacred books; —it claims farther that as a whole they contain a revelation from God. Here again is a broad

distinction between them and the books of the
Chinese religions.   I need hardly speak of the
books of Tâoism.   The Tâo Teh King, which
is the only written document we have from Lâo-
tsze, makes no pretension to be anything but
the thoughtful production of its author.   The
Divine Panorama, from which I quoted largely
in my last lecture, carries on its front the refutation of its claim to be in any sense a divine
revelation.   The classical or Confucian books,
from the Shû down to the Analects, extending
over about 1800 years, and the product of many
different writers, have " no organic unity, no
internal cohesion other than belongs to human
writings produced in the same nation in the
course of many centuries."[1]   It is different with
the writings of the Old and New Testaments,
for Jesus Christ is Himself the theme of them
from the first to the last.   I will not speak of
prophecy in general, though there are prophecies
in the Old Testament about individuals, cities,
and nations, which must have come from Him
to whom " all His works from the beginning of
the world are known."   It is sufficient for me,
in the limits to which I must restrict my remarks,
to insist on the unity of the Bible as proved by

[1] Rogers' " Superhuman Origin of the Bible, inferred
from itself."   P. 162.

its teaching about the person and work and kingdom of our Lord. I believe that all of us have often wished that we had been in the company of the three men travelling to Emmaus on the evening of the day of the resurrection, and had listened to the discourse with which one of them reproved the doubts and cheered the hearts of the other two. You remember how He said to them, " O fools and slow of heart to believe all that the prophets have spoken ! Ought not Christ to have suffered these things, and to enter into His glory ? " And then, " beginning at Moses and all the prophets, He expounded to them in all the scriptures the things concerning Himself." The speaker on that occasion was the risen Lord. He believed in the unity of the sacred writings through their testimony to Himself; and I will assume it therefore as a fact which it is not necessary for me to illustrate any further. In contemplating the fact, we may well adopt the language of the late professor Henry Rogers :— " Shall we say that it is all a dream,—that the book has no such unity, or that all who thought so have gone mad together ? If this be thought incredible, then how shall we account for the delusion ? By chance ? Who can compute the chances against it ? By concert of the writers ?

The mode in which it was constructed, its gradual composition, makes this impossible."[1] To my own mind this unity of the Bible has always appeared "an infallible proof" that it is a book "*sui generis*," in which I am constrained to recognize the hand of God. I must hold that it contains a revelation from Him, and that the religion which it discloses will be different from Confucianism, Tâoism, and the other religions current among men,—different as bearing the stamp of divine authority, and revealing truths to which we could not otherwise have attained.

Bearing of the revealed character of Christianity on the comparison between it and other religions, and on the study of its sacred books.

11. This divine stamp on Christianity must not be supposed to imprint the brand of falsehood on other religions. They are still to be tested according to what they are in themselves. We will approve what is good; we will note what is defective; and we will disapprove what is wrong. The study of them continues to be a duty, full of interest and importance. The results of it will throw light on the religious

[1] Superhuman Origin of the Bible, p. 171.

nature and wants of man, and show how adapted
Christianity is to supply those wants and satisfy
that nature. They will even help to give us, I believe, a better understanding of Christianity itself,
and a more vivid apprehension of its doctrines.

The divine stamp, however, rebukes the view
of some that, by the study of the Chinese and
other religions, we shall find one truth of importance here and another there, and that, bringing
these together, we may by an eclectic process
frame a universal religion that will supersede
Christianity itself. I must think that the
comparative study of religions will dissipate
this imagination, and prove it to be an unsub-
stantial hope.[1]

It must be borne in mind also that when
we have concluded that Christianity is the
revealed religion, this does not relieve us from
the task of searching the scriptures diligently,
and finding out their meaning by all legitimate
methods of criticism and interpretation. The
books of the Old and New Testaments have
come down to us just as the Greek and Roman
and Chinese classics have done, exposed in
the same way to corruption and alteration, to

[1] See two volumes on "Oriental Religions and their
Relation to Universal Religion." By Samuel Johnson
(Boston, United States).

additions and mutilations. The text of them
all has to be settled by the same canons of
criticism ; the meaning of the settled text has
to be determined by similar or corresponding
processes of construction. The fact that we
have in the Christian scriptures a revelation
does not affect the method of their study.   I
shall be told that they were inspired, and I
freely grant that they were so ; but this only
requires from us the stricter and more reverent
adherence to rule in finding out what they say.
I have never formulated to myself a theory of
inspiration.   I know it by its effects, and I
fail to see how, in accordance with what our
Lord said to Nicodemus about the operation
of the Spirit, it can be known in any other way·
Any inquiry, however, into the manner of its
communication lies outside the subject of which
I am treating ; and I hasten to complete the
comparison, or what we must now call the
contrast, of the Chinese religions with Christianity.   Some of you may think that, since
I began to speak of the peculiarity in the
disclosures of the future by Christianity, I have
been digressing from the proper business of the
lecture.   It seems otherwise to myself.   I had
taken nearly all the topics with which the
description of Confucianism and Tâoism supplied

me, and compared them with the teachings of Christianity. The course pursued had brought us into contact with the supernatural event of the resurrection of Christ, as alleged in the New Testament. It was necessary to consider the evidence for it, and we were led on to touch on the claim of our sacred books generally to be received as the oracles of God. I felt that if we accepted the fact of the resurrection and allowed the inspiration of the Bible, it would be necessary thenceforth to contrast any other points in Christianity which the former lectures suggested to me with the silence or all but silence of the Chinese religions on the same subjects. Such has been the logic of my mind in the line of argument and illustration which I have followed, anxious that my treatment of the three religions should be perfectly fair, and as complete as a single lecture would permit. I will only further call your attention to the Christian doctrines of propitiatory sacrifice and future punishment.

The Christian doctrine of the death of Christ as a propitiatory sacrifice.

12. Towards the close of my first lecture, I observed that the oblations at the worship of God in the great religious services of the Con-

fucian religion were thank-offerings, and not propitiatory sacrifices ; and that not even the idea of self-consecration or self-dedication on the part of the worshipper was symbolised by them. It was pointed out that the idea of vicarious substitution was not unknown in very early times in China. T'ang the Successful, and Tan the duke of Châu, were both prepared to die, the former for all the people, and the latter, in lieu of his brother, for the good of their dynasty.[1] Similarly, all along the course of time, on occasion of great calamities, a feeling of their own feebleness has been awakened in the Chinese government and people, and a conviction that their sufferings were a punishment for their wickedness. The sovereign, as the representative of the people, has humbled himself at such times under the mighty hand of Heaven, made confession of unworthiness and guilt, declared his repentance, vowed a more complete devotion to the discharge of his duties, and asked for forgiveness and relief. But this has taken place, still takes place, only on special occasions, when the deep places of the soul are broken up by the blows of affliction and trouble ;—the idea of propitiation or expiation is not found in the regular worship of Confucianism.

[1] Pp. 54, 85.

During the period embraced in the work called "The Spring and Autumn," many covenants were made among the feudal princes,—made over the blood of a victim, with which each covenanting party smeared the corners of his mouth, while an appeal was addressed to the invisible Powers to inflict vengeance on all who should violate the conditions agreed upon. Such a sacrifice might be called **imprecatory.**

The sacrificial offerings at the worship of ancestors are simply the materials of a feast, at which the living and the dead are supposed to meet together.

The Tâoist services to the dead may be called **deprecatory.** Their object is to please or appease the spirits of the departed. They are not, as in Confucianism, the expression of filial piety by surviving children and relatives, seeking in this way still to manifest itself to the deceased and maintain communion with them; but they are on the contrary sacrifices made to avert evil,—to give relief and deliverance to the suffering or tortured ghosts indeed, but still more to save the offerers from the spite that will be wreaked on them, if they do not task themselves to the utmost to perform whatever may be required of them on behalf of the dead.

Thus in the religions of China there is

nothing corresponding to the idea of propitiatory sacrifice as unfolded in our scriptures. The sacrifices prescribed by the laws of Moses have been divided into that of self-consecration or dedication, symbolised by the burnt-offering ; those of thanksgiving, represented in the meat-offering and peace-offering ; and those of expiation, in the sin-offering and trespass-offering. There underlies all these forms of sacrifice the idea of a close relation between men and God. His we are and Him we ought to serve, so that in all our doings of mind and body we should be living sacrifices, devoted to Him. Life and all its blessings are His gift to us, and hence there are due to Him the sacrifice of praise continually, the fruit of our lips, and the ardent love and gratitude of our hearts. But we are far from loving and serving God as we ought to do. We are under the dominion of a carnal mind that is enmity against Him, and refuses to be subject to His law. The more we retain the consciousness of our ideal selves, and the apprehension of what we ought to be towards God and towards our fellow-men, the more deeply and acutely do we realise our unworthiness and guilt, the more ready are we to exclaim, " O wretched men that we are ! who shall deliver us from the body of this death ? "

Here comes in the sacrifice of expiation,—that which was symbolised by the sin and trespass offerings of the laws of Moses, that which was offered on Calvary when Christ bore our sins in His own body on the tree and died, the just for the unjust, bringing us to God. By the sacrificial death of Christ the wall of separation between the Holy God and sinful men is removed; the handwriting of ordinances that was against them is blotted out, and nailed to the cross, where it hangs fluttering and showing to the moral universe how mercy has triumphed over justice, and justice has been glorified and made more august thereby.

It has been said to me that Paul and the other apostles did indeed look on the death of Christ in this way as sacrificial and atoning, but that they took this view of it from their Jewish training, and could hardly avoid doing so, while we need not regard it as more than the greatest instance and example of self-consecration. Bishop Butler in his "Analogy of Religion" has dealt with this representation. "Whereas it is objected," he says, "that all this"—the reference to Christ as a priest and an expiatory victim—"is merely by way of allusion to the sacrifices of the Mosaic law, the apostle on the contrary affirms that the law was a shadow of good things to come, and not the very image of the things (Heb. x. 1); and that the priests that offer gifts according to the law serve unto the example and shadow of heavenly things, as Moses was admonished of God, when he was about to make the tabernacle : 'For see,' saith he, 'that thou make all things according to the pattern showed to thee in the mount' (Heb. viii. 4, 5) ; *i.e.*, the Levitical priesthood was a shadow of the priesthood of Christ, in like manner as the tabernacle made by Moses was according to that showed to him in the mount. The priesthood of Christ and the tabernacle in the mount were the originals ; of the former of which the Levitical priesthood was a type, and of the latter the tabernacle made by Moses was a copy. The doctrine of the epistle, then, plainly is, that the legal sacrifices were allusions to the great and final atonement to be made by the blood of Christ; and not that this was an allusion to them." The view that bishop Butler thus substantiates is but one conclusion from the organic unity of which I spoke as running through the books of Scripture, and proving them to be a revelation from God.[1]

[1] "The Analogy of Religion," Part II., ch. v., "Of Redemption by a Mediator." Bishop Butler accepted the

The operation of this doctrine, the sacrificial death of Christ, is most powerful and beneficial. In the strength of it I draw near to God. He is still to me the holy and righteous upholder of all moral government, but I have ceased to fear Him as vengeful and inexorable, for herein He commendeth His love, giving up His Son to die for sinners; and with faith in Christ there comes into my breast peace with God, and the Spirit of adoption through whom I cry to Him, "Abba, Father." It is no apprehension of an arbitrary forgiveness that relieves me from the sense of sin, and enables me to rise superior to the threatenings of the law :—I am a new creature in Christ Jesus; His death is my most powerful stimulus to a holy life. As from the first Adam I derived a natural life and a carnal mind, so from Christ, the second Adam, I derive a spiritual life, to develope by the help of the Holy Spirit into likeness and conformity to Him.

Such is an imperfect exhibition of the nature and operation of the death of Christ; the little that I have said about it may suffice for my purpose of comparing or contrasting the Chris-

Epistle to the Hebrews as having been written by Paul; but the question of its authorship does not affect the value of its evidence, so long as we receive it as canonical.

tian system with Confucianism and Tâoism. As I have remarked more than once, neither of these religions knows anything of propitiation or expiation in their sacrifices. The knowledge of God in Confucianism, which has become a heritage of the Chinese people, is very precious ; but the restriction of the worship of Him to the sovereign has prevented the growth and wide development among them of a sense of sin. The doctrine of the goodness of human nature, again, may be held so that it shall not conflict with the teaching of our scriptures on the same subject, but its tendency is to lead the scholarly class to think too highly of themselves as capable, unhelped from without, of all virtuous achievement, and to resent the suggestion that our religion is better than their own. There is, in a word, no bringing down of God to men in Confucianism in order to lift them up to Him. Their moral shortcomings, when brought home to them, may produce a feeling of shame, but hardly a conviction of guilt. Tâoism, as a system of superstitions, is antagonistic to Christianity ; but where its professors confine themselves to the study of the Tâo Teh King, and cultivate the humility and abnegation of self which are there so strongly inculcated, they are more prepared than the Confucian literati to receive the message of the gospel. So I found it in the case of one Tâoist dignitary who visited me in Hong-kong, when he was more than fourscore years old. He told me that his study of the tâo of Lâo-tsze for fifty years had convinced him of his impotency to attain to its ideal, and he had almost resigned himself to despair, hopeless of finding some truth for which his heart yearned. Some Christian tracts were brought to the monastery on the hill of Lo-fâu over which he presided. " I read them," he said, " and it was as if scales fell from my eyes." He accepted at once the revelation of God in Christ. Of all the Chinese whom I met with in my long missionary experience he was the one most "prepared for the Lord." He reminded me of the aged Simeon, who had remained long in Jerusalem, waiting for the consolation of Israel, and who saw at last the Lord's Christ.

The sacrificial death of Christ is of the essence of Christianity. It is the disclosure of this doctrine in our scriptures that constitutes the gospel the " good tidings of great joy to all people." It produces at once contrition for wrong-doing, and proclaims the promise of pardon. It tells men how low they have fallen, and how high

they may rise. It tears but only to heal; it
smites but only to bind up. Confucianism and
Tâoism teach nothing at all akin to it. " Herein
is love," writes the apostle John ; " not that we
loved God, but that He loved us, and sent His
Son to be the propitiation for our sins." No
Confucian or Tâoist writer has ever had such
facts to make known to his countrymen. In
this respect there is no comparison between the
religions of China and ours. The advantage is
all with Christianity.

Because the idea of propitiation is unknown
in those religions, they have, as we have seen,
no priests. The emperor is the minister of
religion for all the Chinese people in the worship
of God ; the "yellow Tops" are the ministers
of superstition in the services of Tâoism. Sin-
gularly, just because of the propitiatory sacrifice
in Christianity, there is no peculiar priestly class
or order in it. So far as the eucharistic and
self-dedicatory sacrifices of Mosaism have their
significance in Christianity, all believers are
priests to present them to God, and the death
of Christ should ever inspire them to be doing
so with alacrity. But the propitiatory sacrifice
of Himself was offered by Christ once for all
on the cross. He is our great High Priest,
the only Priest of His Church, the one Lamb

of God who was slain, ever appearing in heaven in our behalf. I do not despise governments in the church. The ministry of the word— I do not read in the New Testament of the ministry of the sacraments—is a most important function, to be discharged becomingly and in order by men apt to teach, but any priesthood of a class, distinct from the priesthood of all believers, would be a derogation from the sole glory belonging to Christ, the one Mediator between God and men.

The Christian doctrine of future punishment.

13. I come to the last subject to which it is necessary, according to the scheme of the lecture, to call your attention in comparing the religions of China and Christianity. That subject is the doctrine of future punishment. But for what I related, in the last lecture, of the recent teaching of Tâoism concerning its purgatory and hell, I might have been tempted to avoid this topic, but I should have incurred in that case my own condemnation for not completing the task which I had undertaken.

Confucianism, as we saw, says nothing about future punishment. The good are rewarded by Heaven and the bad are punished; but the

reward and punishment both take place in the
sphere of time as the natural or providential
results of conduct. The good pass at death
into some state of conscious existence, where
they may be happy, being in heaven, and they
are occupied with the care of the same concerns that interested them on earth ; the bad,
so far as we have any witness about them,
have the same experience. It is with them
after death just as it is with the good. If the
reward due for well-doing and the punishment
due for ill-doing were not all received by the
individuals in their lifetime, there remains a
floating balance of happiness and honour or
of suffering and shame, hid away somewhere, to
be paid over in providence to their descendants
respectively. This is all that Confucianism
teaches about future retribution. We cannot
accept it as a sufficient theory of life, death, and
futurity. If the good and bad live on in the spirit-
world, after their places on earth know them no
more, we refuse to believe that it will be just
the same with them. The harvest of the crops
whose seeds were so different must be different.
It is a Chinese saying, as it is common among
ourselves, that "what a man sows he shall also
reap," but there is no testimony in Confucianism
of the operation of the law after .death. If it

did not continue to operate after death, we should loathe life. It would not be worth living. We should feel that we were the sport of a fantastic and unprincipled fate. The attempt to supplement this lame account of the issues of conduct to the individual by handing over the unsatisfied balance of his experience to his posterity affords the mind very poor satisfaction. Confucius has no revelation of the future that satisfies the longings of the soul or the instincts of our moral nature, or that is sufficient to guide our steps in the way of peace and holiness while we are upon earth.

The teaching of Tâoism on the subject was the same as that of Confucianism at the time when its treatise on "Actions and their Retributions" was published, and continued to be so until the views exhibited in the "Divine Panorama" were adopted. According to that production, there is now an easy ascent to the land of the Immortals by the performance of good deeds, and the orderly regulation of the life; but "the good are few and the wicked many." Hence after death there are for the latter the tortures of purgatory and manifold transmigrations, and to those whom these fail to reclaim there are after all the everlasting torments of hell. Purgatory and transmigration were borrowed by Tâoism from Buddhism ; and I will only say of them that the doctrine of transmigration arose from a wish to account for the different conditions of human life, as happy or miserable, by the character of a former life, of which, however, there is an entire oblivion ; and that the tortures of purgatory are the punishments of sin, obliterating the score of guilt, before the individual enters on his new trial for the eternal future. The new and gentler methods of dealing with the guilty initiated by Yü Hwang and the infernal Powers, as published in the "Divine Panorama," are preceded by the avowal that the methods previously prevailing had been too severe ; which is really a confession that up to that time men had been dealt with unjustly. What are we to think of a system that is not ashamed to make such an acknowledgment ? We despise it, and wonder that anything so weak should have currency even in China. The way in which the author of the treatise gloats over the details of the purgatorial torments is revolting. His reference to a hell beyond was probably taken, as I said in the last lecture, from fragments of Christian books that had fallen into his hands, and were understood by him according to the nature of his mind, filled with the

indigenous superstitions of his system and the
Buddhistic ravings about purgatory.

What now is the teaching of Christianity
about future retribution?

i. It teaches that God has appointed a day in
which He will judge the world in righteousness by Jesus Christ, His Son, our Saviour and
Lord.

ii. As preparatory to this judgment there
will be a general resurrection of the dead. All
that are in their graves shall hear the voice of
the Son of God and come forth. In what body,
with what form, they shall appear, we are not
told, save that it will be a spiritual body, a fit
vehicle for the immortal spirit, and not a natural
body of flesh and blood like the present; and
in the case of those to be approved, it will be
fashioned like to the glorious body of the
glorified Redeemer.

iii. Thirdly, after the resurrection, the judgment will be held. It will serve not only to
determine and make manifest the characters of
men, but will also vindicate the moral government of God in all the course of time, and with
reference to the earthly lot of every individual,
as well as to all the events of history, great and
small. The wisdom and goodness of His providence will be brought forth as the light, and its

righteousness as the noonday. The reverence
of faith, which rested in things that it could not
trace or understand, as being " for the glory of
God," will now give place to the joy of sight,
and find in what was most perplexing occasion
for adoring praise.

The result of the judgment to all who are
gathered at the great tribunal will be,—" glory,
honour and peace to every man that wrought
good, to the Christian first, and also to the
heathen ; but tribulation and anguish on every
soul of man that did evil, on the Christian first,
and also on the heathen." Christians enjoyed
the full revelation of God's will and grace ;
heathens, less highly favoured, yet having the
work of God's law written in their hearts, were
a law to themselves. All will be accepted or
disallowed " according to what they had, and
not according to what they had not." There
will be both heathens and those who were called
Christians in the two companies on the right
hand and the left of the judge ; the approved
or righteous, and the disapproved or condemned.
Then finally, " these shall go away into ever-
during punishment, but the righteous into ever-
during life." Such are the words of the Judge
Himself, the faithful and true Witness, of Christ
whom we believed when He testified of His

own coming resurrection, and whom I must similarly believe when He testifies about the future retribution.

I believe that the above is a fair exhibition of the teaching of Christianity on the subject of retribution ;—different from the silence of Confucianism, and from the revelling of Tâoism over its purgatory and hell. We are looking at it now on its dark side—what it says about future punishment, solemnly declared to be " ever-during " as the life of the righteous. Not a few in our days are offended by this saying. Some protest against it defiantly as "hard" and intolerable, and are ready to go away and walk no more with Christ. Others, who feel that they can go to no other, set about reducing the gravity of His language, and try to show that the scriptures do not necessarily teach " ever-during punishment." May I be allowed to refer to some of my own mental exercises on the question? I had thought and conversed about it, while a student at our most northern university nearly fifty years ago ; but when I had finished my course there, and. while still very young, was launching out into the world, it was brought pointedly before me in a letter from a most valued friend in 1835. He told me that he was writing on the subject

20

of future retribution, and asked if I could adopt the view of universal restoration. I remember the day when, and the desk where, I wrote my reply:—"The end of the present dispensation will be the general judgment; and Christ Himself said that the issues of it would be ever-during life and ever-during punishment. Until I receive an additional revelation, therefore, and am assured that a new dispensation of grace has been instituted, I consider that I am precluded from discussing universal restoration or any other speculation about the future state contrary to the generally received doctrine." That was my view forty-five years ago, and it is my view to-day. Some of my ministerial brethren here have read, I suppose, more books treating of the future retribution than I have had time or opportunity to do, but I doubt whether any have thought about it more than I have done. What books I have read have not unsettled my faith, or loosened the hold of my soul's anchor in its old mooring ground. If the resources of the Almighty Father shall hereafter develop a scheme of universal restoration, I shall be prepared, and have reason, with all the redeemed in heaven, to hail it as worthy of its Author. The scheme of conditional immortality I cannot away with, nor harmonize in any way with my reading of the Bible, and my idea of God as wonderful in counsel, mighty in working, and grand in love. But, as I have just said, it is not for me at the close of this lecture to discuss any view of future retribution different from what the loving Christ declared. On the ground of that He exhorted His hearers, while they had the light, to walk in it, and His immediate disciples appealed to men in such words as—"How shall we escape if we neglect so great salvation?" The subject is both too high and too deep for us. There may be possibilities and impossibilities in it, which we are unable to comprehend at present. Instead of doubting or denying, it is more seemly for us to receive the revealed word with the meekness of faith. God, the Righteous and Holy, will do what is right; Christ, the Friend of sinners, will conduct the processes of the judgment. What more would we have? What more can we get? We judge no one, but I am sure that existence will not have an unhappy issue to any child of man who has not "judged himself unworthy of everlasting life." For eternity, as for time, Christianity is the best religion, the only religion that bears on it the stamp of divine authority and completeness.

I must now draw to a close the exposition of

the themes which I undertook to bring before you. I have done my work as fully as I could in the compass of four lectures, and cannot be sufficiently thankful for the patience with which you have listened to me. If I have in any degree misrepresented either of the religions of China, I can safely say that the fault has been unintentional.

Practical Issues of the four Lectures.

13. I said that I would call attention in conclusion to two practical issues to which the lectures should lead. Let it suffice for me to do little more than mention them. What I have said about Confucianism and Tâoism shows us the need that there is in the great empire of China for Christianity. During my long residence among the Chinese, I learned to think more highly of them than many of our countrymen do ; more highly as to their actual morality, and more highly as to their intellectual capacity. Their best attainments in moral excellence, however, are not to be compared with those made by docile learners in the school of Christ. The true Christian is the highest style of man. And now that the wall of partition that separated China from other nations has been thrown down, I believe it is only their adoption of Christianity

that will enable the people to hold their own, and lift them up in the social scale. China is a chosen field, perhaps I might say *the* chosen field, of the English Presbyterian Church. You have had, and you still have, most efficient missionaries there,—men distinguished among their compeers of other churches by a singular tenacity of purpose and devotedness of life. Their success has been great. You began, and have thus far continued well; let nothing hinder your going forward. The harvest truly is great, but the labourers are few. I pray the Lord of the harvest that He will, by your instrumentality, send forth a multitude of labourers into that greatest of earth's mission fields.

The other practical issue is that these lectures should stimulate us all to prove our personal Christianity by the untiring exhibition of the Christ-like attributes of character and by our earnestness in all Christian work. If Christianity have not triumphed in the past, if it be not triumphing in the present, in a way likely soon to bring on the state for which Christ taught us to pray,—that the will of our Father may be done on earth as it is in heaven, what is it that withholdeth? Let us not say that God's purpose slumbers, that His hand is

21

shortened, or His ear heavy; let us not doubt
that Christ has all authority in heaven and in
earth. We must blame ourselves:—the divisions
among Christian churches; the inconsistencies
and unrighteousnesses of professors; the selfish-
ness and greed of our commerce; the ambitious
and selfish policy of so-called Christian nations.
I cannot illustrate what I mean better than by
telling you, as my last word, of a conversation
with His Excellency Kwo Sung-tâo, the former
Chinese ambassador, soon after he arrived in
London in 1877. "You know," he said to me,
"both England and China. Which country do
you say is the better of the two?" I replied,
"England." He was disappointed, and added,
"I mean looking at them from the moral standpoint;—looked at from the standpoint of benevolence, righteousness, and propriety, which
country do you say is the better?" After some
demur and fencing, I replied again, "England."
I never saw a man more surprised. He pushed
his chair back, got on his feet, took a turn across
the room, and cried out, "You say that, looked
at from the moral standpoint, England is better
than China! Then how is it that England
insists on our taking her opium?"

Hazell, Watson, and Viney, Printers, London and Aylesbury.

Printed in the United States
24172LVS00003B/136-156